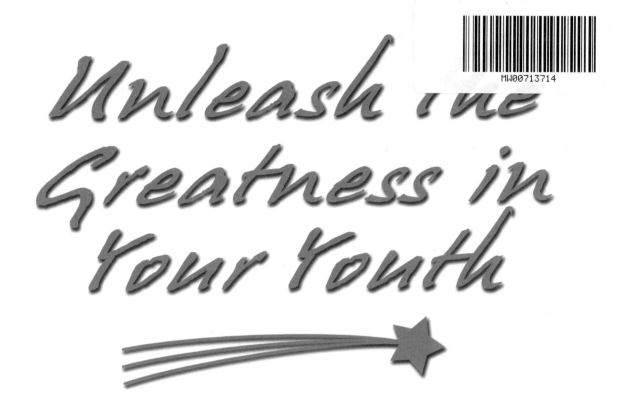

Unleash The Greatness in Your Youth

Powerful,

Character–Building,

Positive

Parenting Activities

An "I Care" Positive Parenting Workbook

No part of this "I Care" *Unleash the Greatness in Your Youth* Workbook may be reproduced in whole or in part, or stored in a retrieval system, or transmitted in any form or by any means electronic, mechanical, photocopied, recorded, or otherwise without express written permission of the publisher, "I Care" Products & Services.

Schools and school systems **do not** have permission to copy any part of this book for use as instructional material. Each Workbook is intended for individual use.

All of the logos, artwork, designs, and activities in this Workbook are exclusively owned by "I Care" Products & Services and are protected under copyright law.

Written by Elbert D. Solomon and Martha Ray Dean
Book design and artwork by Phillip L. Harper, Jr. and Valerie Hines

ISBN: 978–189118–717–9
6th Grade; First Edition
Copyright© January 2007 by "I Care" Products & Services
E–mail: parents8@icarenow.com
www.icarenow.com/parents.html
All rights reserved. Printed in the U.S.A.

Table of Contents

Introduction

The "Unleash the Greatness in Your Youth" Workbook

The activities in this *Unleash the Greatness in Your Youth* Workbook are built around many of the foundational concepts and skills your soon–to–be teenager will need. Highly successful individuals share a number of traits in common. Among them are the thinking skills, attitudes, and behavior patterns that represent "character." This book provides tools for parents like you who want to begin unleashing the potential in their children through the development of their character.

Positive Parenting

Positive parenting strengthens parent/child relationships by engaging young people with the most important teachers they will ever have—their parents. Furthermore, it increases academic achievement and expectations for the future; instills self–esteem and confidence; and reduces behavior problems and school absenteeism.

Character Development

Character development doesn't just happen, it is primarily learned from role models and significant adults and should be started at an early age. But it can't stop there. Research shows that even though middle school students may challenge authority from time to time, they rely on their parents for what to do in difficult situations. They are also watching what parents do all the time and notice if parents don't practice what they preach.

"I Care"

Since its beginning over ten years ago, "I Care" has been committed to three principles: 1.) Focus on character development, which influences all aspects of a child. 2.) Get and keep parents involved, which also impacts all aspects of child development. We do this by communicating the importance of parental involvement. 3.) Making "I Care" a bridge between school, home, and community—better results come from teamwork. Today, "I Care" is used by over a million parents.

"I Care" Positive Parenting and Mentoring Curricula

"I Care" Positive Parenting and Mentoring Curricula are used in over 60,000 classrooms for toddler and pre–K through high school. Activities similar to the ones in this workbook are implemented by parents throughout the school year. Administrators, teachers, and parents have all raved about the results.

Feedback

Feedback is one of the key components to the "I Care" approach. Defining parental involvement as the number of positive interactions you have with your child makes it easy. The *Reflection Log* Activity at the end of each month will help you keep track of your involvement. The other indicator will be the changes you see in your youth. They will be stunning.

Practice, Practice, Practice

Read through the month's activities together and decide on the ones you want to do. You can fit them into your schedule at any time. Remember, practice is necessary for a behavior or attitude to become a habit. That's why we provide so many activities for each character trait. In fact, learning theory tells us that it generally takes 21 days of practice before a new habit is acquired. But don't stop with ours! Be creative in developing your own activities as well.

Discuss, Discuss, Discuss

Discuss—not tell, tell, tell—is the rule. All learners need to talk about an idea using their own words, ask questions about it, and consider it from different points of view to both learn it and understand it more completely.

Monthly Character Traits

There are twelve important character traits, one for each month of the year, spiraling from a *Pillar of Character*. They instill self–esteem, positive attitudes, and self–confidence. Focus on one character trait per month and complete the *Talk About It*, do activities together, get your child involved in service, review the positive message, and complete the reflection activities.

Strengthen Your Understanding

At this age, most youths have personal interests. Thus, one key to motivating them is to help them pursue their interest areas. The activities in this section include: writing, reading, art, music, teamwork, computer work, projects, and performances. No matter what your child's interest or ability, he will find something to interest him. Do as many of the activities as will fit into your schedule, five or more at least each month, to help the learning sink in.

Service Projects

Research shows that youths who spend at least one hour a week helping others are less frequently involved in destructive behaviors and do better in school than their peers. The youths themselves say that volunteering helps them develop leadership skills, learn patience and kindness, and understand what good citizenship is all about. Even though service projects take more time and planning than other activities, they are worth the effort.

Scenarios

Scenarios ask you to imagine what you might do in certain situations. The practice they provide is valuable in preparing a child to make the right decisions in everyday life because he has thought about what he might do ahead of time. When he actually finds himself facing a dilemma, he has a better chance of knowing how to handle it.

Connect! Connect!

At the beginning of each month, have your child look over the section called *Connect! Connect!*. It lists films, books, and web sites related to the trait you'll be talking about. Movies can help you start talking about a character trait, and most films are available through video rentals. If the library doesn't have a book he's interested in, they can borrow it for you from another library.

Positive Affirmations

Affirmations are positive sentences that describe what you want your life to be like. You repeat them many times by saying them aloud, thinking about them or writing them down so they go deep into the subconscious mind and affect what you think and do. The more you repeat the affirmation, the more you believe it. It is very important to choose only positive affirmations. If negative thoughts creep in such as, *"I can't do this,"* replace them with the positive affirmation. There are affirmations for both parents and youths. Repeat them frequently to each other and to yourselves. They can also be hung up where you can see them every day.

Positive Messages

Visual reminders are as helpful for middle–schoolers as they are for toddlers. Post the monthly *Positive Message* where your youth can see it often and go over it together.

Reading Activities

Reading daily is beneficial no matter how old you are. It helps brain development, improves writing skills, increases our knowledge, stimulates our imagination, and gives us pleasure. You might want to designate a family reading time during the week, if not daily, where everyone is reading. Recommended books may be available at your local library. Or, you may purchase a set of 12 books—one for each month—at www.icarenow.com/parents.html. These are appropriate for 6th grade readers. However, some 6th grade readers read far above or below grade level. If your child is one of these, we can provide you with a list of books at his reading level. If you're not sure what your child's reading level is, ask his teacher.

Reflection Log

The monthly *Reflection Log* Activity is designed for parents to summarize their positive actions, recognize their accomplishments, and encourage self–initiation of more positive parent/child interactions. Begin thinking about activities they might do in the future.

Tips for Parents

From time to time, we all need a little help with parenting challenges. In this section, you'll find suggestions for setting expectations, sharing your personal experiences, getting the whole family involved, serving as a role model, and communicating with your young adult. Specific activities and discussion topics are listed for you to choose from.

Message to Student

As children enter adolescence, they're interested in acting older and winning the approval of their peers. They become more observant and they think more about the kind of person they want to be. The information and questions in this section can help get them thinking about what the trait of the month means and how well they are already using it—or not using it. It also includes suggestions on what they need to develop the trait.

- Built on twelve universally recognized pillars of good character with spiraling grade–level character traits to build one behavior on another
- Include the primary behaviors that define each character trait for the repetition that enables transfer of learning
- Include parenting/mentoring, enrichment, reinforcement, visual learning, and reflection activities
- Additional workbooks will soon be available for all the grades listed below

Pillar of Character	6th	7th	8th
Motivated	*Planner*	*Focused*	*Priority Conscious*
Reliable	*Virtuous*	*Follows Through*	*Truthful*
Persistent	*Push Personal Limits*	*Productive*	*Proactive*
Peace Keeper	*Cooperative*	*Withstands Peer Pressure*	*Tolerant*
Self–Control	*Responsive to Feedback*	*Self–Disciplined*	*Cautious*
Caring	*Dependable*	*Empathetic*	*Generous*
Responsible	*Willing to Accept Blame*	*Problem Solver*	*Aware of Consequences*
Civic–Minded	*Humanitarian*	*Service Oriented*	*Conservationist*
Communicator	*Express Feelings*	*Listener*	*Public Speaker*
Confident	*Positive Thinking*	*Makes Right Choices*	*Bold*
Respectful	*Appreciate*	*Polite*	*Fair*
Self–Knowing	*Sets Personal Standards*	*Calm*	*Thoughtful*

A Proven Educational Method

"I Care" follows best strategies of the teaching and learning process described below and has been professionally developed using relevant research.

Positive Psychology

The focus of psychology has traditionally been on what's wrong with people and how to fix them. Recently, however, some psychologists have begun to look at the strengths and virtues in people that make them happy and protect them from mental illness and depression. They believe that if traits such as courage, optimism, kindness, hope, honesty, and perseverance can be developed in young people, they will grow into happy adults who make a positive contribution to society. "I Care" is a pioneer in the development of positive, character–building curricula and workbooks.

Three Essential Learning Conditions

These have been identified by cognitive psychologists and embedded into the workbook: reception, availability, and activation.

1. Reception—Advanced organizers focus the child's attention on specific activities.
2. Availability—Parents can take advantage of the "teachable moments" and insert parenting activities into the home schedule at any time.
3. Activation—When parents role model the character traits and ask questions such as those provided in the pre–planned activities, they are activating the child's cognitive assimilation of the trait.

Open–Ended Questions

An open–ended question is one that requires some thought to answer. It usually begins with "why," "explain," "what do you think about . . . ," or "what if . . . ." It allows room for more than one right answer and encourages more details, more analysis, and more creativity. This is especially important to adolescents who are self–motivated.

As you discuss some of the activities, you have an opportunity to praise your child for the effort he puts into his thinking, even if you might not completely agree with his ideas. Remember that this is the age at which young people are trying to find out what they believe. As much as they are aware of their own changing bodies and feelings, they are also becoming more concerned with the feelings and rights of others. Whether they will admit it or not, they listen to what you say and carefully watch what you do.

Connected to Real Life

Adolescents really like to be doing things and not just thinking or talking. That's one reason they respond so well to activities that relate to their own experiences. Let them interact with peers or get them involved in helping others. When they see how traits like self–control, setting standards, or honesty make them more successful in everyday life, these traits are more likely to become life–long attitudes and behaviors.

Knowing some of the changes your adolescent will experience, as well as the attitudes and behaviors he might display, will help you keep the lines of communication open with him. Here are some of those behaviors your adolescent may begin to exhibit:

Intellectual Growth

- Begin thinking more about the future
- Try using humor, such as sarcasm, more in conversation, pointing out inconsistencies in what people say and do
- Have more curiosity about the world (though they may be disinterested in traditional learning)
- Develop new interests (but may not stick to them)

Social Growth

- Seek out peers with whom they have things in common to increase their sense of security
- Want more freedom and power to make their own decisions and resent when they don't get them
- Withdraw from physical affection in the family (though they still want and need it)
- Talk back to adults more as a way of asserting their independence

Moral Growth

- Identify more with the underdog and disadvantaged, desiring to improve their situations
- Begin forming their own opinions of right and wrong that may differ from those of the family
- Are still dependent on parental guidance because logical reason is not fully developed
- Begin questioning social conventions and the way things are done

Emotional Growth

- Focus on themselves and how others see them
- Feel self-conscious about the physical, social and emotional changes they are undergoing
- Experience mood swings which they don't understand
- Make decisions based on desire to fit in rather than whether or not they are the best decisions

Physical Growth

- Go through rapid and uneven growth spurts that make them self-conscious
- Have periods of sleeplessness and restlessness due to changes in hormones
- Need physical activity to channel increased energy and restlessness
- Can be awkward and uncoordinated because of uneven growth

As children enter adolescence, it's not unusual for a parent to think: "Who is that in my son's body?" or "This isn't the same girl who lived here last week." Keeping up with all the changes that are taking place will help you stay connected with your son or daughter and make it easier to communicate. We suggest that before you begin working on any of the activities in this workbook, you spend a little time getting acquainted with the person your child is becoming. The questions below can help you get started. Talk them over with your child and encourage detailed responses. Answer a few of them yourself. Listen and learn. Afterward, use what you learn to modify activities to your child's interests and abilities.

- What are some of the problems in the world that you would change if you had the power to do so? Why is that so important to you? What about the problems in our community?

- There's nothing like talking to someone in person to get to know them. Imagine you have the opportunity to spend an hour with anyone in the world. Who would it be? Why that person? What would you ask him or her?

- Do you think your interests have changed in the last few years? In what ways? Do you like the same kinds of music and movies? How about friends? What do you think caused you to change?

- Thinking about the future, what three things would you really like to do well?

- What careers would you like to know more about? Why do they interest you?

- If you were being interviewed for a summer job that you really wanted and you were asked to describe the things you do really well, what would they be?

- Pick a city that you'd like to visit—one you've never been to before. What are the things that you would like to do there?

- What would you like people to understand about you that they don't seem to?

- What are the things that make you sad, happy, confused, curious, and mad?

- Picture yourself about to receive an award for your latest book. What is the book about?

- What is your favorite musical group? Relative? Place to visit? Color? Memory?

- For a school project you will be working on a video about homeless people. What job would you want—such as planning, directing, interviewing, or photographing?

Source: *The Interest–a–Lyzer*, Joseph S. Renzulli, Creative Learning Press

Talking with Your Adolescent

One recent survey of young teens showed that 75% were worried about getting along with their parents. One of the most important things parents can do to assure a good relationship with their adolescent is to listen when he talks, respect his opinion—even if they don't agree with it— and include him in making decisions. The following topics are ones that adolescents and teens want to talk about with their parents:

Family decisions: Adolescents are very observant. They know when something's up. Whether it is planning a vacation or planning a divorce, they want to know about it. Talk with them about family plans. Discuss pending decisions, ask for their input, and explain your position, especially if it concerns them.

Sensitive issues: Adolescents are curious and sometimes confused about their changing bodies and feelings. They're encountering topics about which they may need guidance. Don't try to protect your adolescent from issues you think he's too young to understand, or issues you might not feel comfortable talking about, like sex, drugs, or alternative lifestyles.

You: What you think and feel, as well as what you experienced when you were young are all interesting to your child. They're especially interested in the life challenges you had at their age and how you dealt with them.

What's happening in the world: Current events are thrust upon us from the television screen and the computer screen 24/7. The tone in which much of it is reported creates concern in adolescents who don't have all the facts or don't realize that just because an event is being talked about all the time, it's not necessarily a common occurrence. Discuss their concerns and help them find answers to their questions.

The big whys: Adolescents are beginning to think beyond what happens to why it happens. Why is there so much hate in the world? Why do people think only about their own needs and wants and not about others? Your answers to these kinds of questions may be based on your religious beliefs or what you believe about people. Whatever your beliefs, share them with your child.

Them and their future: If you are really interested in what your child likes, thinks, and does, she knows it. She also knows when you're not interested, and that makes her feel less worthy. Talk with your child about the things she likes to spend time doing. Talk about her friends. Discuss some of the things she will encounter when she goes to high school and what her thoughts are about a career and how she wants to live her life.

Source: www.teentouch.org

Parents Do Make a Difference: How to Raise Kids With Solid Character, Strong Minds, and Caring Hearts, by Michele Borba

Michele Borba is a national expert on building children's self–esteem, achievement, and motivation. In this book she focuses on the role of parents in character development, helping them understand some of the foundational behaviors necessary for their child's success. Included is advice on how to encourage these behaviors, suggested activities, resources for parents and children, as well as lots of examples.

Building Moral Intelligence: The Seven Essential Virtues that Teach Kids to Do the Right Thing, by Michele Borba

In this book, Michele Borba takes the foundational behaviors she discussed in *Parents Do Make a Difference*, and examines each one in greater depth. She provides a test for parents to assess their children on these behaviors, suggests activities, and advises parents to make sure they are providing a moral example that they would want their children to follow, or in other words, watch their own behavior.

The Power of Positive Talk: Words to Help Every Child Succeed, by Douglas Bloch with Jon Merritt

This books starts out by explaining how words can shape the way children behave, both good and bad. Using lots of examples the author illustrates what positive talk is and how children can use it in the situations they encounter—for instance, learning, athletics, or peer relationships. For each situation, he gives an example of negative self–talk and how to turn that around with positive affirmations. With the user–friendly format, you can find suggestions at the spur of the moment without having to wade through pages of text.

WHY Do They Act That Way? : A Survival Guide to the Adolescent Brain for You and Your Teen, by David Walsh

Some of those frustrating behaviors we see in adolescents are brain–based. This book explains those changes going on in the adolescent brain so that parents can understand, communicate with, and stay connected to their kids. Numerous illustrations show why moodiness, quickness to anger and to take risks, miscommunication, fatigue, territoriality, and other familiar teenage behavior problems are so common.

Helping Boys Succeed in School, by Terry Neu and Rich Weinfeld

Compared to girls, more boys drop out of school and fewer boys go to college. This book provides parents and teachers with ideas for channeling boys' interests, keeping them involved in school and home, and helping them deal with some of the unique social and emotional problems boys face. It includes advice to boys from other boys, strategy checklists, and case studies that illustrate what works.

I Pledge to Teach My Youth How to Be:

Motivated

Reliable

Persistent

A Peace Keeper

In Control of Self

Caring

Dependable

Civic–Minded

A Communicator

Confident

Respectful

Self–Knowing

Tear out this page and display the Parenting Pledge on the other side in a visible location.

I Pledge to Be:

A Planner

Virtuous

A Role Model and Push Personal Limits

Cooperative

Responsive to Feedback

Dependable

Willing to Accept Blame

A Humanitarian

A Role Model and Express Feelings

A Positive Thinker

Appreciative

A Role Model and Set Personal Standards

Tear out this page and display the Youth's Pledge on the other side in a visible location.

What's It All About?

Planning is one of the most important things we can do. It can mean the difference between success and failure. Planning a meal, planning a vacation, planning a party, planning a project, planning how to sell an idea to your boss, planning a budget, planning your future—the list is endless. If we learn how to plan, and do it often enough, it will become automatic. We'll do it without thinking about it. That's what you want.

Good planning saves time and money. It keeps you from wasting your energy and resources. It also prevents little problems from becoming big problems.

Message to Parents

How often do you plan? Did you think about what you needed to do today or for the week? If so, great; if not, why? Planning is easy for some people. For others it can be a challenge, perhaps because they aren't in the habit or because they are what's called a "random thinker." Some of us are "concrete thinkers" who think in sequential steps and some of us random thinkers. Our ideas jump around. No matter how you think, you can find a way to plan that's right for you.

Planner

Message to Student

> Planning is the process by which you work out the most effective way of reaching your goal.

How Am I Doing?

Ask yourself the following questions. If the answer is yes to all or most of them, you are probably planning pretty well. If you seldom or never do them, you could learn a lot from the activities this month.

◇ When I need to get something done, I think about how to schedule my time.
◇ I make a list of the resources or equipment I need.
◇ I know the steps I need to reach my goal.
◇ My goals—what I want to accomplish—are really clear to me.

Making Some Changes
How To Develop This Trait

Check out the steps of good planning in the example below. You will have a chance to use them with many of this month's activities.

1. Write your goal.
2. Describe how you will know you have reached it.
3. List the activities that will get it done.
4. List the resources you need, including people.
5. What's your time line—who does what by when?
6. Implement the plan.
7. Evaluate the results.
8. Celebrate your accomplishment.

Tips for Parents

Being Role Models

◇ Work with your child to develop the habit of planning for the next day the night before. Do it every day for a week and evaluate how helpful it was. Discuss the importance of writing out your ideas so some of them aren't forgotten, because we can only hold seven pieces of information in our minds at once. You can use the steps for good planning on page 2 to get you started. Examples: what to wear, what should be done before school, transportation needs, etc.

◇ Have a family meeting to talk about plans for a future event. Discuss priorities and reasons behind options and choices. Include your child in making the plans. Examples: special dinner for the extended family, weekend To–Do list, how to spend an upcoming holiday, etc.

◇ Help your child plan and give a party for family or friends. Use the steps for good planning. Even if you don't need it, your child will benefit by walking through all the steps.

Talking It Over

◇ Discuss with your child the following sayings:
- *If you fail to plan, you plan to fail.*
- *"To achieve great things, two things are needed: a plan, and not quite enough time."*—Leonard Bernstein
- *Bad planning on your part does not constitute an emergency on my part.*
- *A good plan today is better than a perfect plan tomorrow.*

◇ Talk with your child about something each of you did last week that would have worked out better with more planning. Did you forget something or waste time because you hadn't thought about what you needed to do or what you needed to take with you? Talk about the problems avoided by planning. Examples: wasting time and effort, failing to consider all the factors, forgetting some necessary resources, forgetting important steps, doing more than you need to, etc.

Strengthen Your Understanding

Youth Instructions: There are companies that sell what are called "day planners," notebooks that have a page for each day of the year where you can write down what needs to be done that day. They also make planners for businesses to write down their goals for the year and month, then make a list of the actions needed to reach the goals. Some businesses hire consultants to train the employees how to plan. That's how important planning is to them. Go to www.franklincovey.com and click "Paper Planning Systems" under "Shopping." Check out the different kinds of planning pages, then, along with your parent(s), create a planning journal of your own design. Keep track of what you need to do during the month—projects, school assignments, people to contact, etc. At the end of the day, you can check off what was accomplished and make a note of what needs to be done the next day.

Youth Instructions: Many kids are planning projects of their own these days—inventions, investigations, informing people about problems or issues, and helping others. They are finding that good planning helps them reach their goals. Read the descriptions of some projects at www.kidscare.org, search "News Corner." Talk about the kinds of planning the kids had to do to be successful.

Parent Instructions: Are there any event planners in your community? Wedding planners, party planners, meeting planners at hotels and restaurants? Encourage your child to call one and set up an interview. He can ask such questions as:

◇ How did you get interested in planning as a profession?
◇ What special training did you need?
◇ What steps do you always use when you are planning an event?
◇ What advice do you have for me about becoming a better planner?

Strengthen Your Understanding

Parent Instructions: Imagine with your child what it would be like to design an "extreme adventure," something that is challenging, seldom done, and takes place somewhere most people don't go. Some examples might be sea kayaking in Patagonia (*Where's that? Look it up.*), exploring the coastline caves at the tip of New Zealand, or digging for pirates' gold on the outer banks of North Carolina. Each of you plan what you would do if money were no problem. Describe what you know about the location and the challenges you would have to overcome. Plan what to take, how to get there, with whom you would go, as well as necessary safety arrangements. Share your adventures with each other. Did you plan well? Did you think of all the necessary equipment? Was it transportable? How about health and safety precautions? Do you think you'll ever take a trip like that? Why or why not?

Parent Instructions: *Saving Lilly* by Peg Kehert is a book with a message about mistreated animals. In it, the main characters plan a way to draw attention to this problem. After reading the book with your child, discuss something he feels passionately about and what he might do about it. Help him plan how to carry out his mission.

Youth Instructions: A brain map is a picture of the brain that shows which part controls what we do and what happens in our bodies. There is a part of the brain that controls seeing, hearing, taste, smell, and touch, for instance. The frontal lobe is the part that controls planning. You can actually exercise your brain to keep mentally sharp and even improve your thinking skills. Research shows that activities like Bingo, reading, traveling, listening to music, doing math problems, and solving riddles are all beneficial for brain development. Watching television is not. Go to www.rinkworks.com/brainfood/ and try out some riddles. Remember, it's helping develop your brain so you can plan better.

Strengthen Your Understanding

Parent Instructions: Planning is important both short–term (things that will happen soon), as well as long–term (things that may not happen for years). One example of long–term planning that is too often neglected is retirement income. Go over the following statistics about retirement planning with your child:

◇ *32% of people working today say they haven't saved at all for retirement.*

◇ *Most people think they will work beyond retirement age, so they don't think they have to save as much. However, 40% of retired people today retired early, half because of health problems.*

◇ *Someone now earning around $30,000 will need annual retirement income of between $19,500 and $25,500. Most people who have retirement savings have just over $100,000 total. How long will that last?*

Discuss reasons that people put off this kind of planning and the consequences they face as a result.

Youth Instructions: After watching what happened during Hurricane Katrina, many families are planning ahead for emergencies. Go to www.ready.gov to learn about some of the emergencies your family might face and what to do about them. Review the kinds of planning they recommend, from knowing how you will be able to find each other, where to go, what should go into an emergency kit, and personal information everyone will need. Spend a Saturday with your parent(s) gathering the information and supplies. Make your plans and make sure everyone knows what they are.

Youth Instructions: Storyboards were first developed by Walt Disney for the purpose of planning the sequence of scenes in animated movies. They looked like a giant comic of the movie and helped directors and cinematographers make decisions about whether the story was complete and how to mesh the sound track to the animation. Today, storyboards are used by authors planning scenes in stories and novels, cartoonists and comic book creators, and filmmakers and reporters planning a story for television. Select an issue of which you want to make others aware. It may be the environment, safety, peer pressure, hunger, or homelessness. You can sketch the main shots, points, or pictures in sequence, one per box, then write down the dialogue that would go along with the shot. You can find some examples at www.thestoryboardartist.com, use the storyboard frames on page 7, or make

Strengthen Your Understanding

Planner

Service Opportunities

◇ Brainstorm with your child ways he can help some senior citizens in your community. Ideas might include: cleaning their house or yard, writing letters for them, keeping them company, sharing a talent at a senior center or nursing home, or arranging for transportation. Have your child select a project that interests him and plan the steps for carrying it out. In addition to planning, he will have to decide if the project is really doable. He may also have to raise money to get it done. Help him when he needs it until the goal of the project has been met.

◇ The possibilities are endless!
  • Draw pictures to brighten the hospital rooms of young children.
  • Collect and donate books and toys to homeless shelters.
  • Accompany handicapped peers on outings.
  • Campaign to save an endangered animal or adopt a zoo resident.
  • Ask students to recycle gently worn toys and clothing for a needy child.

Scenarios

What Would I Do in This Situation?

Dad said you could go camping with him this weekend if you finish your science project that is due Monday. You also have to finish cleaning the garage. How are you going to fit it all in?

You really want to be on the varsity basketball team when you go to high school. What are some of the things you need to do to prepare?

Connect! Connect!

Media/Video

◇ Yep, *Without a Paddle* is a story of three buddies who run into one dilemma after another because they—didn't plan. Watch the video, and after you're finished laughing, talk with your child about times you each got "caught" because you didn't think ahead.

◇ Talk about the need for planning! In the *Swiss Family Robinson*, a shipwrecked family must figure out how to survive in a strange land with no food and very little in the way of provisions. Talk with your child about how well your family would survive in a similar situation. How could you develop the imagination needed to meet the challenges?

Books, Web Sites, and Other Resources

◇ **Book of the Month:** *Saving Lilly* by Peg Kehret: In a reading competition, Erin Wrenn's class earns a field trip to the circus. At the circus, Erin observes Lilly, an elephant, being mistreated by some of the performers. She urges her classmates to earn $8,000 to buy Lilly so she can be sent to an elephant sanctuary. The class raises the money by washing cars, mowing lawns, and other odd jobs. In the book, planning helps Erin and her classmates work hard and achieve their goal.

◇ *Athlete's Guide to Career Planning* by Delight Champagne, Judy Chartland, Steve Danish, Shane M. Murphy, and Albert J. Pitipas: This book provides specific tools for making important life decisions for someone planning an athletic career. Reviewers actually recommend it for young people interested in sports.

◇ *Clever Party Planning* by Suzanne Singleton: Chock full of fun ideas, this book is a great family resource and talks about all the things you need to plan for when having a party.

◇ www.redcross.org: Here's a site with information on planning for emergencies. Check it out!

Planner

Positive Message

"If you know where you are going, you will take the right road to get you there.

—Elbert Solomon

Reflection Log

Summarize your child's positive interactions during the month and reward yourself for a job well done.

Child's Name _____ **Date** _____

Name of Parent(s) _____

Record the number for each of the following questions in the box on the right.

A. How many of the workbook activities did you do with your child? ☐

B. How many positive recognitions about your child did you receive from teacher(s)? ☐

C. How many positive recognitions did your child receive from family members, friends, etc.? ☐

D. How many positive recognitions did your child receive from you, the parent(s)? ☐

Planner

Positive Activities

D. Record five self–initiated positive activities you did with your child that were not in this month's workbook activities.

1. _____

   _____

2. _____

   _____

3. _____

   _____

4. _____

   _____

5. _____

   _____

Copyright© 2007 "I Care" Products & Services (6th Grade)

What's It All About?

Virtue is something that has been talked about for thousands of years as character traits that lead people to do good. If you have a combination of wisdom, courage, kindness, justice, and mercy, you are considered a virtuous person.

Virtue is knowing the difference between right and wrong, and choosing to do the right. In a permissive society such as we have become, there is less agreement on what is right and what is wrong. But, if you're going to teach others about virtue, you need to decide for yourself what is right and what is wrong.

Message to Parents

Why is there less emphasis on right and wrong than there used to be? There are many reasons, but one is that most parents don't teach it. One juvenile court judge asks young offenders, *"Did anyone teach you the difference between right and wrong?"* The overwhelming response is, *"No,"* yet these young people come from "good" families. Why then aren't parents teaching them?

Some are too busy. Others don't know how. Some talk about it, but don't live it themselves, so their children ask, *"Why bother?"* Whatever the reason, it's time for parents to ask, *"What kind of person do I want my child to be?"*

Virtuous

Message to Student

" Doing the right thing because it is the right thing: that's being virtuous. "

How Am I Doing?

Ask yourself the following questions:

◇ Do you do things you don't want other people to know about?
◇ Do you lie to get out of trouble?
◇ Do you go along with what your friends want to do so they will like you?
◇ Are you ever rude and disrespectful?

Making Some Changes
How To Develop This Trait

◇ Challenge yourself to do the right thing even when your friends don't.
◇ Use the 10 second rule: count to 10 before you say or do something when you are upset. Let your brain kick in so you can think about whether what you're about to say or do is a good idea.
◇ Ask yourself:
  ▪ Is this a good idea?
  ▪ What is good about it?
  ▪ What harm can come from it?
  ▪ Would _____ do it? *(Put the name of someone you respect into the blank.)*

Tips for Parents

Being Role Models

◇ Virtue is something that is caught, not just taught. That means your child will learn more from what you do than from what you say.

◇ Point out to your child anyone who is an example of virtue.

◇ Use self–talk to point out the good things you do: *"Mrs. Jonah is in the hospital, so I'm taking dinner to the family so Mr. Jonah doesn't have to worry about it. My mother taught me to help out people in need."*

◇ Praise your child when she exhibits a specific virtue. *"That was a wise thing to do."*

◇ When your child makes bad decisions, acknowledge them: *"You didn't tell the truth about what happened. We don't lie in our family. Tell me why you did."*

Talking It Over

◇ Discuss with your child ways in which she can say *"no"* when someone—whether it is a best friend or stranger—tries to get her to do something wrong.

◇ Share with your child a time when you made the choice to do the right thing and how that was a good choice. Example: *"Some kids were copying right from the book when writing reports. I didn't because I knew it was wrong, and I had to do lots of writing later in school and needed the practice. I got good at writing."*

◇ Discuss with your child the following sayings:

  ▪ *What is virtue? It is to hold yourself to your fullest development as a person and as a responsible member of the human community.*

  ▪ *All we need for evil to prevail is for good people to do nothing.*

Virtuous

Strengthen Your Understanding

Parent Instructions: Discuss with your child how standing up for what you believe can be unpopular, and no one wants to be rejected. This was true when millions of Germans said nothing as Jews were transported to the concentration camps and killed. It is true when injustice anywhere goes unchallenged. Taking a stand for what is true and right (not just different) is bold. It takes courage. Those are people who should be admired. Talk with your child about something that she'd be willing to take a stand on even if it made her unpopular. If she can't think of anything, ask why.

Parent Instructions: Ask your child to write a profile of someone she considers a really good person. What personal characteristics does the person have that make him so good? Why or why not? Also, have your child discuss whether she considers herself virtuous.

Youth Instructions: Look up the word *virtuous* in a dictionary. Brainstorm a list of behaviors that a virtuous person possesses. Example: "*A virtuous person is conscientious, honorable, incorruptible, ethical, good, and upright.*" See if you can fill the page. Then, go back and check off the behaviors that describe you some or all of the time. Circle the ones you want to work on.

Strengthen Your Understanding

Parent Instructions: With your child, read several opinion editorials from the newspaper. Then, ask her to write an editorial on why virtue is important for 6th graders. She can even send it to the paper.

Youth Instructions: Every time in history has its good and bad. Looking back, we realize how bad slavery was, for instance. Fortunately, there were virtuous people who stood up against it. What are some of the bad things happening today? Who are the people standing up and saying it is wrong? Does everyone agree about what needs to be done? Why or why not? What might people say about this in 100 years?

Parent Instructions: Read *The Girls* by Amy Goldman Koss with your child. Discuss how virtue can cause others to reject us, why this happens (because others feel less worthy) and what we can do about it (say positive things to those who are rejecting us).

Virtuous

Strengthen Your Understanding

Youth Instructions: Studies of 37 different languages turned up seven words that have very similar meanings. They are: joy, fear, anger, sadness, disgust, shame, and guilt. Six of the seven describe negative emotions. Studies also show that most people talk about these negative emotions most of the time. All this negative talk influences people's attitudes and behaviors. With your parent(s), make a list of the kinds of negative words you hear a lot. What effect do they have on you and others?

Parent Instructions: Watch one of your child's favorite television shows with her. Were the characters good role models of virtue? If not, should your child be watching it all the time? What about other shows she watches? Use television as a teaching tool. Challenge the facts and behaviors of the characters if they do or say negative things. Having a collection of good videos is an alternative to negative TV, or try the video rental store or public library.

Parent Instructions: The generation of World War II has been called "the greatest generation" because of the sacrifices they made for freedom. They practiced virtue without making a big deal of it. Arrange for your child to interview someone from this generation. Have her write her questions ahead of time, such as, *"How have people's beliefs and behavior changed since you were my age?"* Be sure to take pictures and record the interview. Ask your child to write a summary of what she learned to give to the person she interviewed. She might even want to do more research about why the generation was so great.

Strengthen Your Understanding

Parent Instructions: You can talk to your child about making good choices for only so long, then you have to give her the freedom to choose. When she asks you if she can do something she knows she shouldn't, but won't stop bugging you, say, *"I've taught you right from wrong and raised you to be responsible, so you know what, you make the decision."* (as long as safety is not an issue). She'll be shocked, but chances are she'll make the right decision. If she doesn't, don't say *"I told you so."* Let the consequences speak for themselves.

Parent Instructions: Almost every day, there are examples in the news of famous people breaking the law or behaving badly. They are setting a bad example for everyone. Talk with your child about why the government, businesses, and even families have "codes of conduct" that explain how they expect people to behave. Also, talk about why some people ignore codes of conduct, and what should happen when they do.

Virtuous

Service Opportunities

◇ Create a "How to Stay Safe" flyer to give to the kids in your school and neighborhood. Decide if you want to make it for kids your age or younger. Collect safety tips from books and the internet. You could even interview a police officer about what you should include. Make it interesting to look at and easy to read. Distribute flyers wherever you can. How has doing this project changed you? If it didn't, why is that?

◇ School teachers can always use help because they have so much to do. Volunteer to help out in an after–school program or day care. You could read to the younger children. If that isn't possible, ask the teacher if you can make letter or word flash cards for beginning readers. She'll be able to find something for you to do. What did you learn by watching the reactions of the children?

Scenarios
What Would I Do in This Situation?

Jack is mad because he got detention for skipping class. He's trying to convince Dana to help him vandalize the principal's car. What should Dana do?

It's a fact: a student's report to a principal led to the arrest of two Wisconsin teenagers recently. When police searched the teens' homes, they found guns, knives, and ammunition. The student reported hearing one of the teens threaten to attack the school. What would you do in that situation?

Copyright© 2007 "I Care" Products & Services (6th Grade)

Connect! Connect!

Media/Video

◊ *Sky High*: Sky High is the first and only high school for kids with superhuman powers. Will must use his newfound superpowers to save the day and prove himself a hero worthy of the family tradition. If you were a super hero, what problems would you solve?

◊ Virtue is the theme of such hero movies as: *Superman, Spiderman, Robin Hood, and Ivanhoe*. You can also watch any John Wayne movie, such as *True Grit* or movies about World War II to see how people's true natures come out under pressure.

Books, Web Sites, and Other Resources

◊ **Book of the Month:** *The Girls* by Amy Goldman Koss: This is a story about peer pressure and cliques that every adolescent can relate to. The events in this story will make you pause before you think about changing who you are to fit in.

◊ *Shabanu: Daughter of the Wind* by Suzanna Fisher Staples: Shabanu, a young Muslim girl, is called upon to sacrifice everything she's dreamed of to uphold her family's honor. Will she do it—or listen to the stirrings of her own heart?

◊ *Among the Hidden* by Margaret Peterson Haddix: Luke is the third child in his family. The law says each family is allowed only 2 children, so he's been hidden for 12 years, until a stray glimpse through an air vent reveals his existence. Talk about whether there is anything you believe in strongly enough to risk your life for.

◊ *The Book of Virtues for Young People* by William Bennett: This collection of morality–based tales illustrates a wide variety of virtues.

◊ www.mcgruff.org: This is the web site of McGruff, the Crime Dog. Kids and parents can find advice on staying safe.

Virtuous

Positive Message

" Virtue does not come from wealth, but . . . wealth and every other good thing which men have . . . comes from virtue.

—Socrates

February

22
Do Not Photocopy.   Copyright© 2007 "I Care" Products & Services (6th Grade)

Reflection Log

Summarize your child's positive interactions during the month and reward yourself for a job well done.

Child's Name _____ **Date** _____

Name of Parent(s) _____

Record the number for each of the following questions in the box on the right.

A. How many of the workbook activities did you do with your child?

B. How many positive recognitions about your child did you receive from teacher(s)?

C. How many positive recognitions did your child receive from family members, friends, etc.?

D. How many positive recognitions did your child receive from you, the parent(s)?

Virtuous

Positive Activities

D. Record five self–initiated positive activities you did with your child that were not in this month's workbook activities.

1. _____

_____

2. _____

_____

3. _____

_____

4. _____

_____

5. _____

_____

Copyright© 2007 "I Care" Products & Services (6th Grade)

What's It All About?

Did your parents ever say to you, *"You'll never know if you can do something if you don't try."*? 99% of the time they were right. We are all able to do more than we think we can. Pushing your limits means working extra hard to do something you didn't think you could do or working to get better than you've ever been. Olympic athletes are a good example. They set goals and work to achieve them. But, pushing your limits is not just trying harder, it is also trying something you have never done before. One way to find out what you're really capable of is to try new things and not give up.

Message to Parents

There are so many distractions in today's culture—media, technology, peer pressure—that it's not unusual for young people to "coast by" without putting much effort into their work. Many of them have never tested the limits of their abilities because they don't have any personal goals. To set the stage for a discussion of this month's trait, it might be helpful to discuss what inspires athletes, musicians, or race car drivers to push their limits. On the other hand, some children become perfectionists, wanting to do everything right. You won't need to encourage them to push their limits. You may need to assure them that it's not necessary to push all the time. Then, there are the young people who are always comparing themselves to their peers. Who's developing the fastest, getting taller, stronger, or better–looking? When you talk about pushing your limits, you might want to emphasize that it's not about being better than others, it's about doing your "personal best."

Push Personal Limits

Message to Student

"You don't push your limits to be better than everyone else or to please your parents. Sometimes you do push your limits to get things done, like working extra hard on a school project or so you can get chosen for a sports team. But pushing your limits is more than that. You do it so you can discover what you can do. One way to find out what we are really capable of is to try new things and not give up."

How Am I Doing?

Ask yourself the following questions:

◊ Do you do your best, or just get by on school work?
◊ Do you know when you're not doing your best? Do you know why?
◊ Do you avoid trying new things because they might be hard?
◊ Do you try to make things better and people happier?
◊ Do you ever think about who you are and things you want to do in life?

Making Some Changes
How To Develop This Trait

◊ Imagine yourself doing something you've never done but want to do, or doing something better than you do it now.
◊ Start small. Someone learning to run a marathon race starts by running short distances at first. They run a little further every week until they can run the distance of the entire race.
◊ Practice a lot.
◊ Believe in yourself.

Tips for Parents

Being Role Models

◇ People who become really good at a sport, a job, as a friend or student usually have a role model who inspired them. What kind of role model are you? Do you push your own limits? Have you been coasting for a while? Let your child see you setting goals for yourself that help you push your limits.

◇ Use self–talk, talking to yourself as you are working, to let your child know that you are challenging yourself to do something that is difficult. Comment on your frustrations and your sense of accomplishment.

◇ Encourage each member of your family to pick one thing they'd like to do better. Talk together about what each of you can do, and then do it.

Talking It Over

◇ Talk with your child about how "pushing your limits" can be important if someone has a handicap.

◇ Many athletes try to perform at their "personal best." Talk with your child about what this means. Is it what he is doing now, or what he could do if he really tried? How do athletes achieve their personal best?

◇ What does it mean to push the limits of what is acceptable?

◇ Discuss the following quotes with your child:

  ▪ *Push your limits far enough, and you'll find you don't have any.*

  ▪ *You can push your limits, but to be the most productive possible, know when enough is enough.*

Push Personal Limits

Strengthen Your Understanding

Parent Instructions: When the Spanish explorer Hernando Cortez landed in Veracruz in the sixteenth century, the first thing he did was burn his ships. *"Men,"* he told his crew, *"you can either fight or you can die."* What he did by burning the ships was prevent the men from turning around and sailing home. The point is that sometimes it is necessary to make a serious commitment to pushing your limits so you don't turn back. Discuss with your child how he can ask people to hold him accountable to help him keep pushing his limits.

Parent Instructions: Share with your child an example of something you thought you couldn't do, but after trying it found you were able to do it after all. Have your child write down some sayings that remind him to "push his limits" and hang them up where he will see them regularly. Examples include: *"Try harder." "I CAN do it." "If at first you don't succeed, try, try again."*

Youth Instructions: One way to push limits is to try and do a task in a shorter amount of time than usual. For instance, completing math homework, getting ready for school, or running a race. Select something that you will do in a shorter period of time, as long as you does not risk your safety. After you have finished, talk with your parent(s) about whether you can work faster all the time, or whether pushing your limits made you less careful and accurate. There are some things you need to go slow on.

Strengthen Your Understanding

Parent Instructions: Help your child find a biography or article about Christopher Reeve. After reading it, talk about the ways in which he pushed his limits and how many other people benefited from his example.

Youth Instructions: Both you and your parent(s) pick one thing you've never done before—something that would be a challenge like walking a certain distance, trying a new sport, or memorizing poetry. Do it, then talk about whether it was easier or harder than you thought it would be.

Parent Instructions: Talk with your child about people you know who have pushed their limits. Help him arrange to interview one of them. Think through the questions he could ask, like *"What made you want to work so hard?" "What was the most difficult thing you did?" "How did you keep yourself going?"* After the interview, discuss what he learned that he can use in his own life.

Strengthen Your Understanding

Youth Instructions: Hang up pictures of people who are pushing their limits. You can find some at www.specialolympics.org. Discuss with your parent(s) how people's expectations for what handicapped people can do has radically changed as a result of some "heroes" who pushed their limits. You can also find pictures of athletes, dancers, doctors, firemen, and poets. In any walk of life, you will find people who push their limits.

Youth Instructions: *A Single Shard* by Linda Sue Park is about an orphan boy in 12th century Korea who faces hardships in his struggle to become who he was supposed to be. Read it and discuss with your parent(s) the special qualities that made it possible for Tree-ear to push his limits.

Parent Instructions: Encourage your child to gather friends together and plan a "Personal Best Day." What would be the goal of the day? How could they get other kids to participate? How will they explain what their "personal best" means? How will each person decide what his personal best should be and how would he know if he reached it?

Strengthen Your Understanding

Youth Instructions: Kids who are motivated find they can do things they never thought they could. They started with an idea, like Trevor, who made sandwiches and gave them out to the homeless. Pretty soon, other people were helping and things grew until they had Trevor's Place, where families can live while they are finding a permanent home. It's still running 23 years after Trevor began handing out sandwiches. Check out some other examples at www.kidshelping.org. Then, talk with your parent(s) about how pushing your limits can start with a small idea that grows, and you grow along with it.

Youth Instructions: *Wilma Unlimited: How Wilma Rudolph Became the World's Fastest Woman* by Kathleen Krull is inspiring. It tells the true story of a young girl no one expected to live when she was born, who no one expected to walk when she contracted polio at the age of four, but who became the first woman to win three Olympic gold medals at the age of 20. Talk about the ways Wilma must have pushed her limits to become the world's fastest woman.

Parent Instructions: Did you know the more you read, the better you read—and the better you write? Challenge your child to improve his reading. Each of you select a hard book about something you're already familiar with, or try an easy book on a topic that you're interested in but don't know anything about. Ask a librarian for help finding a book. After you've finished the book, find another that is a bit different and read that one.

Push Personal Limits

Service Opportunities

◊ Is there a Special Olympics near you? You can find out by going online to www.specialolympics.org. Find out about volunteer opportunities. Being around handicapped athletes will provide a great example of people who have achieved beyond their expectations—and the expectations of others. After participating, ask yourself what you've learned by watching handicapped individuals really push their limits.

◊ You can learn things by volunteering that you can't learn in books. You can see people's lives change and problems get solved. You make friends you might never meet. You learn new skills. Many people even discover what they want to do with their lives. But the first time you volunteer can be a little scary because it's such a new experience. Talk with you parents about something you'd like to learn about through volunteering, like finding homes for abandoned animals, setting up a recycling program in your school, serving as a companion for a handicapped child, or conducting a food drive for a homeless shelter. While you are serving as a volunteer, keep a journal of what you have learned, what you wished you'd known, what your most memorable experience was, and how you feel the experience changed you.

Scenarios
What Would I Do in This Situation?

Volleyball is really big in your school and everyone plays it. Your friend has been complaining that he feels left out because he just can't play volleyball, but you've seen him and you know he hasn't really tried. What would you say to him to help him understand about pushing his limits?

Your teacher has given an assignment that you just don't think is fair because you have to do so much in a short time. Not only do you have to research a less developed country, you have to present the information to the class in a way that will interest them. You've never done that before. How would pushing your limits help you successfully complete this project?

 Copyright© 2007 "I Care" Products & Services (6th Grade)

Connect! Connect!

Media/Video

◇ *Racing Stripes* is a fun family movie about a barnyard zebra who dreams of winning the Kentucky Derby but doesn't realize he's a zebra. How does he push his limits and go beyond what most zebras do?

◇ *Miracle* is a true story about a hockey coach who pushed his team to win an Olympic gold medal over the Russians who had dominated the field for 20 years. Talk with your child about times when it is important to push beyond what you think you can accomplish. Also, discuss some of the consequences.

Books, Web Sites, and Other Resources

◇ **Book of the Month:** *A Single Shard* by Linda Sue Park: Tree–Ear, a young orphan in the 12th century, becomes interested in the pottery trade after becoming the potter Min's helper. Throughout the story, Tree–Ear faces many obstacles that force him to push his limits.

◇ *Bear: Heart of a Hero* by Scott Shields and Nancy West: Bear was named Hero Dog of the Year for his search and rescue work at the time of 9/11. He's an example of how animals push their limits to help their masters.

◇ www.specialolympics.org: Children and adults with intellectual disabilities who participate in the Special Olympics develop improved physical fitness and motor skills, greater self–confidence, and a more positive self image.

◇ www.chrisreevehomepage.com/biography.html: After visiting this web site, talk with your child about the courage it must take for handicapped people to do what doctors tell them they will never do.

Push Personal Limits

Positive Message

" *Our greatest weakness lies in giving up. The most certain way to succeed is always to try just one more time.* "

—Thomas Edison

Reflection Log

Summarize your child's positive interactions during the month and reward yourself for a job well done.

Child's Name _____ **Date** _____

Name of Parent(s) _____

Record the number for each of the following questions in the box on the right.

A. How many of the workbook activities did you do with your child?

☐

B. How many positive recognitions about your child did you receive from teacher(s)?

☐

C. How many positive recognitions did your child receive from family members, friends, etc.?

☐

D. How many positive recognitions did your child receive from you, the parent(s)?

☐

Push Personal Limits

Positive Activities

D. Record five self–initiated positive activities you did with your child that were not in this month's workbook activities.

1. _____

   _____

2. _____

   _____

3. _____

   _____

4. _____

   _____

5. _____

   _____

Copyright© 2007 "I Care" Products & Services (6th Grade)

What's It All About?

We are a culture of diversity, where everyone values his freedom to do and be what he chooses. One of the problems with this is that people don't cooperate with each other as much as they used to because they want to do things their own way. That's too bad because research has shown that working together to achieve a common goal produces higher achievement and greater productivity than working alone.

It's the same with cooperative learning. When people work on a project as a group, most of the group show higher–level reasoning, more new ideas and solutions, and greater transfer of what is learned within one situation to another than when they are learning alone. But being cooperative is more than that. It means we want to share not only the work, but also information, ideas, and the pleasure of a job well done or are willing to share the responsibility when things don't turn out as planned.

Message to Parents

Psychologists report that one of the biggest worries parents have is how to get their adolescent child to cooperate. Psychologists also say that one of the first things they ask parents is whether family members are concerned about each other, spend time together, and discuss daily events and things that interest them; or do family members seldom talk, and when they do, are they angry and arguing? One of the best ways to get adolescents to cooperate is to be a good communicator. Give your child your full attention, don't interrupt when she is talking, and let her know you really want to understand. When your child knows you're listening, she'll tell you more and listen better when it's your turn to talk. If your child refuses to cooperate, use an "if . . . then" agreement. *"If you get the dishes done quickly, then we can watch the show you want to see."* This puts the responsibility on your child. She has a choice to make and she knows what will happen if she does—or does not—cooperate.

Cooperative

Message to Student

> Think about the following saying: *I may be standing up on the outside, but I'm still down on the inside.* Does that ever describe you? Cooperation is more than doing the right thing. It is an attitude in your heart that says I *want* to do what is right *because* it is right, not just because someone told me to do it.

How Am I Doing?

Ask yourself the following questions:

◊ Do you ever mutter under your breath, sigh, or roll your eyes when you are doing what your parents tell you to do?

◊ How do you react when your parents don't let you do everything you want to do?

◊ Do you put off doing your homework and chores until your parents nag you into doing them? Why do you do it?

Making Some Changes
How To Develop This Trait

◊ Pay attention to what people say.

◊ Think about why it is important to do something instead of why you don't want to do it.

◊ Do your best in whatever you do.

◊ Take turns when several people want to do the same thing—or when no one wants to do something that needs to be done.

◊ Include everyone.

◊ Thank others for what they do.

Tips for Parents

Being Role Models

◇ Are you a model of cooperation when your child is not around? Does she hear you complain about having to cooperate with co–workers and family members? If so, you may need to think about your own attitude—or explain why you think your complaints are justified—if they are.

◇ Model cooperation for your child in the ways you respond to her. For instance, tolerate more silence, as kids sometimes need longer to formulate their ideas. Don't become aggravated by a short attention span.

◇ No one learns cooperation without someone to cooperate with. Keep your child involved with family and friends. A bored teen is an unhappy teen, and unhappiness leads to frustration, and frustration to withdrawal.

Talking It Over

◇ Discuss the following with your child:
  - *"A single arrow is easily broken, but not ten in a bundle."*—Japanese proverb
  - *"It is better to have one person working with you than three people working for you."*—Dwight D. Eisenhower
  - When would it be wrong to cooperate with someone?
  - What's the difference between being cooperative and just going along with a group?

◇ Have a discussion about cooperation in the family. In what ways do you cooperate with each other, and how does that make things nicer? In what ways do you *not* cooperate enough, and how does that make things difficult or unpleasant? Make a "family cooperation" chart and see if you can do something about improving the cooperation within the family.

Cooperative

Strengthen Your Understanding

Parent Instructions: Encourage your child to create and teach a lesson on cooperation for young children. First, she needs to decide what age she wants to work with and make arrangements to teach them. Then, she can go online and search for or draw pictures of cooperation and ask the school librarian for some books she can read for her own information and to her students. Is there a game she can play with them that requires cooperation? Take pictures or video of her teaching and share with family and friends.

Parent Instructions: Try a cooperation activity with your child. Scatter objects on the floor throughout the house but don't let her see them. Then, have her put on a blindfold and verbally guide her through the obstacle course. Let her do the same for you.

Parent Instructions: Do you remember reading the fairy tale *Hansel and Gretel* by the Brothers Grimm? You can find it in the library or online. Read it with your child and talk about how the brother and sister in the story put aside their disagreements, cooperated with each other, and were able to defeat the witch and find their way home. Ask your child to write her own fairy tale about cooperation to share when she teaches younger children.

Strengthen Your Understanding

Parent Instructions: It's a fact: the children of families that sit down at the dinner table together for meals are more cooperative than the children of families that don't. It may be a challenge to your schedule, but try to arrange family meals five times a week, whether at supper during the week or breakfast and lunch on weekends. Use this time to talk to each other.

Youth Instructions: Group activities such as sports are one way to learn cooperation. If you're not interested in sports, how about 4–H, Boys and Girls Clubs, scouts, or a local youth group? Or, there are debate and drama clubs, band or chorus. Service organizations are always looking for volunteers. You can participate in a group activity of your choice.

Youth Instructions: Here's a cooperation challenge for you to do with a friend. Each of you hold one end of a length of rope about 5 feet long. The challenge is for you to tie a knot in the rope without letting go—and without talking to each other. How long does it take?

Cooperative

Strengthen Your Understanding

Parent Instructions: Have your child design and make 20 "Cooperation Certificates," then decide together how she can earn them—perhaps by going out of her way to be cooperative. After she has earned a certain number of certificates, reward her with a special treat.

Parent Instructions: Ask your child to list as many examples of cooperation she observed during the day as she can. Most adolescents may give 4 or 5 examples and stop. Tell her if she can think of 50 examples, you'll give her a "Cooperation Certificate."

Parent Instructions: The next time you have a discussion with your child, both of you practice active listening. It may be awkward at first, but be patient. You'll get the hang of it. Search "active listening" online for some ideas. Pretty soon, you'll be using it in all your conversations. It really improves communication.

Strengthen Your Understanding

Youth Instructions: Security at airports has become strict in an effort to prevent any explosive materials from being taken onto airplanes. Most people are very happy to cooperate with the regulations, but others say they're simply not going to tolerate the new rules. They admit that they ignore the restrictions, slipping expensive cologne, perfume, lip gloss, lotion, and ointments into their carry–on bags or into their pockets in hopes of sneaking them past security. Talk with your parent(s) about the dangers of this kind of *I'll do whatever I want* attitude.

Parent Instructions: Is a dramatic example of the importance of cooperation what your child needs? Then watch *Ladder 49* together. It tells the story of a firefighter who finds his life in danger in the worst blaze he has ever fought. Here, you'll see that cooperation can make the difference between life and death. There is some strong language in the film, but the lessons are worth watching for.

Cooperative

Service Opportunities

◇ The compassion that young people develop as they are involved in serving others contributes greatly to the development of a cooperative attitude. If you have a pet, contact the local retirement home and see if you can take your pet to visit the senior citizens who live there. Or, perhaps there is an elderly person you can "adopt" as an honorary grandparent. Watch and see how much they look forward to your visits.

◇ Gather your friends together and talk about ways you can help the community. Select a project you can all work on. You can find suggestions on how to get started at www.childrenforchildren.org, click "Kids" and then "Plan a Community Project." Projects could include holding a fix–up day to help senior citizens paint and repair their homes, planting trees and flowers in the local park, or volunteering to help people with special needs. For other project ideas, go to www.kidshelping.org or www.geocities.com/HelpfulHandsjr.

Scenarios

What Would I Do in This Situation?

When Hurricane Katrina struck in 2005, there was a big problem—no cooperation between the local, state, and federal governments. But we "average Americans" sure pitched in to help. Imagine that a natural disaster strikes a neighboring state and almost 100,000 are left homeless. Discuss some of the ways you and your family would cooperate with relief agencies to lend a hand. Why is it that most of us aren't so generous and helpful all the time?

Your teacher assigned you to be the leader of a team working together on a group project. Your friend, Clare, was also in the group and wanted to be the leader . She took out her anger on you by not paying attention during team meetings, although she worked really hard on the project so she could get most of the credit. Write a pretend letter to her describing what happened, how it affected the group, and what she might do differently next time to be more cooperative.

Copyright© 2007 "I Care" Products & Services (6th Grade)

Connect! Connect!

Media/Video

◇ *The Goonies*: A group of friends who call themselves the Goonies need to solve a problem: a corrupt corporate developer has bought out their neighborhood and plans to flatten all their homes. The Goonies may be goofy, but their cooperation saves the day. What would you do in their situation?

◇ In *Ice Age 2*, survival is at stake and the animals must help each other to survive. Pick one television program and watch it with your family. Afterward, have a family discussion about things people did in the program that were examples of either good or bad cooperation. Make a list of these examples.

◇ *Cars* is the adventures of one particular car that does not believe in teamwork. What price does he pay because of this? What does his experience teach you about the importance of cooperation?

Books, Web Sites, and Other Resources

◇ **Book of the Month:** *A Week in the Woods* by Andrew Clements: Mark has just moved to a new school, and has no intentions of making friends because he know his family will move again next year. Mark's teacher, Mr. Maxwell, takes his class on a week–long adventure in the wilderness, and as a result, Mark and Mr. Maxwell learn some valuable lessons about judging others.

◇ *The Giver* by Lois Lowry: Is there ever a negative side to cooperation? After reading *The Giver*, talk about the sacrifices that the people of Jonas's world made for it to be perfect. What did Jonas think after he learned the truth?

◇ www.fourhcouncil.edu: Find out if there is a 4–H club in your area. They have great leadership training for young people.

◇ www.bgca.org: The Boys and Girls Clubs of America have lots of after school programs, from sports and the arts to leadership and community service. Enter your zip code to find a club near you.

Cooperative

Positive Message

" *We must be willing to learn the lesson that cooperation may imply compromise, but if it brings a world advance it is a gain for each individual nation.* "

—Eleanor Roosevelt

Reflection Log

Summarize your child's positive interactions during the month and reward yourself for a job well done.

Child's Name _____ **Date** _____

Name of Parent(s) _____

Record the number for each of the following questions in the box on the right.

A. How many of the workbook activities did you do with your child?

B. How many positive recognitions about your child did you receive from teacher(s)?

C. How many positive recognitions did your child receive from family members, friends, etc.?

D. How many positive recognitions did your child receive from you, the parent(s)?

Cooperative

Positive Activities

D. Record five self–initiated positive activities you did with your child that were not in this month's workbook activities.

1. _____

_____

2. _____

_____

3. _____

_____

4. _____

_____

5. _____

_____

What's It All About?

Feedback is information about what we do or say. It is important for building any relationship and getting jobs done because we need to tell people what is working or what isn't working. *"I don't think that's the right box. It won't fit through the door"* is feedback. So is *"I can't hear you when you talk so quietly."* Feedback isn't about whether we are a smart or good person.

To improve, we sometimes need to know what we've done wrong or how we can get better, so it's important to take the feedback that people give us and use it to improve instead of getting mad because we think they are criticizing us.

Message to Parents

◇ At this age, your child is beginning to think rationally and weigh the pros and cons of a situation or decision with greater understanding. His brain hasn't developed this ability to its full capacity. That won't happen until he is in his early twenties, but it begins in adolescence. As a result, he can take information such as feedback and use it to change his behavior. For instance, he can begin to understand that he can influence what people think of him by how he acts.

◇ You may have heard the saying, *Experience is the best teacher*. Sometimes you need to let your child feel the feedback of experience. When you know your adolescent is making a mistake, don't rush in to fix it (unless it's a question of safety). Pick the important issues—constant feedback can become nagging and criticism.

Responsive to Feedback

Message to Student

"A way to really grow is to know what we need to improve. Feedback can help us figure it out. Getting a "C" on a test is feedback that says, *You need to study more.* Applause after scoring a soccer goal is feedback that says *Keep up the good work.* When someone tells you you've done something wrong, do you feel attacked? When you get good feedback, you need to let your brain take over your emotions and say, *"That's good to know. Thanks!"*

How Am I Doing?

Ask yourself the following questions:

◇ When you get an assignment back from the teacher and she said you made some mistakes, do you look over the mistakes so you don't make them again, or do you feel mad and embarrassed and throw the paper away?

◇ Have you ever gotten feedback that helped you? What was good about it? What did you do about it?

Making Some Changes
How To Develop This Trait

Receiving Feedback:
◇ Take a deep breath if you start to get nervous. Smile and look the person in the eye.
◇ Nod your head. That doesn't mean you agree with them; it means you are listening.
◇ Pay attention to the information, not how you feel about it.
◇ Ask for more information if you're not sure what the person is saying.
◇ If you disagree, say, "I'd like to tell you what I think." Then, explain calmly.
◇ If someone is dumping on you, don't interrupt; that starts an argument. Just listen and say, *"Thank you for telling me."*

Tips for Parents

Being Role Models

◇ Practice giving feedback as a family. Make it a learning time. Gather everyone together and say, *"We can all learn from each other. Each person think of one thing he can tell the person sitting next to him that will help that person do something better; for instance, throwing a softball, washing dishes, answering the phone, being on time, keeping promises"*—anything that is helpful and not hurtful.

◇ You have many opportunities to give feedback to your child:
- Following up after you have assigned him a job
- Going over a homework assignment
- Sharing what his teacher said after a conference at school
- How his attitude affects the whole family
- Pointing out how he can improve his basketball or hoop shot

Talking It Over

◇ Practice with your child positive ways to respond to feedback; for example: *"Thank you." "Can you give me more details?" "That's helpful feedback." "How do you think I could do it better?"*

◇ Share with your child some ways in which feedback has been helpful to you in the past.

◇ Discuss with your child how comfortable—or uncomfortable—you each are asking for and getting feedback.

◇ Discuss with your child the following sayings:

- *Would you rather learn from a mistake or keep making it over and over?*
- *"Feedback is the breakfast of champions."*—Ken Blanchard

Responsive to Feedback

Strengthen Your Understanding

Parent Instructions: Relate the following story to your child: *Allison was having a difficult time with her math. At her teacher's suggestion, she started keeping a record of her mistakes. Each week, she wrote down errors she seemed to keep making over and over. After three weeks, she was ready to discuss the mistakes with her teacher.* Discuss what information your child can use as feedback to improve some area of his life. For example, mistakes made when playing his favorite sport, grammar errors made on written assignments, or why he seems to feel angry when someone tells him to do chores.

Parent Instructions: Read *Ghost in the Tokaido Inn* by Dorothy Hoobler and Thomas Hoobler with your child. Discuss the kinds of feedback the Seikei got from different people and how he reacted to it.

Parent Instructions: Encourage your child to make up a form that will help him think about how to use the feedback he gets. It might include questions like:
   ◊   What was the feedback?
   ◊   Have I heard anything like that before?
   ◊   What did I do well?
   ◊   What do I need to improve?
   ◊   How am I going to improve?

Strengthen Your Understanding

Parent Instructions: It is said that Thomas Edison knew 1800 ways *not* to make a light bulb. Christopher Columbus thought he had discovered the East Indies. History is full of people who had failure. Some gave up. Others used failure as a lesson and kept improving. It's the same with feedback. The key is what we do with it. Discuss with your child examples of people who turned failure into success. Other examples are Walt Disney, who was told he never had any good ideas, and Abraham Lincoln, who went into the Black Hawk War as a captain and came out as a private.

Youth Instructions: Make a list of all the kinds of feedback you can think of. Keep adding to it during the month. Talk with your parent(s) about which kinds of feedback you each find most helpful, as well as which kinds make you feel uncomfortable.

Parent Instructions: With your child, think of examples of feedback and criticism for each of the situations below. What's the difference between the two? How would you feel if someone gave you the feedback? How would you feel about the criticism?

 ◇ You're late getting to school because you forgot to put your permission slip in your backpack and had to run home to get it.
 ◇ Jane called Shawn "stupid," which really upset him.
 ◇ Your brother ate your favorite piece of chicken, although it's not his favorite.

Responsive to Feedback

Strengthen Your Understanding

Youth Instructions: Keep a journal for the month, writing down all the different kinds of feedback you have gotten and what it means to you. Examples might be from a sports coach (*"I need to practice my jump shot"*), papers the teacher returns (*"I am creative, but I need to work on my spelling"*), what your friends say (*"they enjoy spending time with me"*), people's body language (*"Josh keeps away from me because he's embarrassed by what happened last week,"* or *"Dave smiles a lot. I think he's starting to feel comfortable in middle school"*), how difficult it is to get up in the morning (*"I'm staying up too late"*). There is an endless source of feedback all around us.

Youth Instructions: Although the words "good job" aren't really feedback because they don't tell us what we did well, we like hearing them. With your parent(s), make a list of as many different ways of saying "good job!" as you can think of. Create a poster with them and hang it up for the family to see.

Parent Instructions: Feedback can come in many forms. After reading *The Landry News* by Andres Clements, talk with your child about the different kinds of feedback in the story and how people reacted to them.

Strengthen Your Understanding

Youth Instructions: Check out the book reviews by kids on www.amazon.com. Select "books" where it says "search" and type in the title *Ghost in the Tokaido Inn* next to it. When you scroll down on the page that comes up, you'll see three reviews written by kids. This is a kind of feedback that helps people decide if they want to read a book. After reading *Ghost in the Tokaido Inn* yourselves, decide if you each agree with the reviews.

Parent Instructions: Have your child write reviews of all the books he reads this month. Search the title of the book on www.amazon.com like you did in the activity above. As you scroll down the page, you'll come to a section called "Customer Reviews." Click the words "Write an Online Review." On the next page that comes up, click "Use Our Kids' Review Forum" and then follow the directions for putting the review on the web site. Also on that page are "Review Guidelines." Ask your child to read and explain them to you (putting them in his own words will help him understand them). He and his friends will enjoy seeing his review online!

Service Opportunities

◇ Young children love to learn from older kids. Do you know any boys or girls who could use your help? Perhaps they need extra encouragement in their school work or just someone to listen to them read. Ask your parents or teachers to help arrange for you to spend some time each week with a younger child. Practice what you will say to encourage them and how you would give them feedback to improve when they need it.

◇ We can't improve if we don't know what's wrong. That's why businesses ask for feedback from their customers. What have you seen in your community that needs to be improved? Is there litter in the public park? Are animals running loose in the streets and yards? Have you noticed a dangerous intersection that needs a stop light? Write a letter to the person or organization that can do something about it. If you don't hear from them, write another or get some friends to send letters, too.

Scenarios
What Would I Do in This Situation?

Your teacher has assigned a 4–person team to work on a project that will be 50% of your grade for the next quarter. One of the team members has missed both times you have met after school, even though he promised to be there. What feedback would you give your team member and how would you say it?

Your teacher just returned a writing assignment that you worked really hard on. She told you that your story was very creative, but your sentences weren't well–written. How do you feel about that? What will you do as a result of the feedback?

Connect! Connect!

Media/Video

- ◇ *The Greatest Game Ever Played*: Find all the different kinds of feedback in this super movie, including the ways that a 10–year old caddy helps Francis become a champion.

- ◇ *October Sky*: This is the true story of Homer Hickam, a coal miner's son who was inspired by the first *Sputnik* launch to take up rocketry against his father's wishes. After seeing the movie, ask your child to point out what was feedback to Homer and what was criticism.

- ◇ *Groundhog Day*: This is a fun family movie in which the main character is a bossy snob who lives the same day over and over again until he finally accepts the feedback he's given and changes his ways. Talk with your child about why some people just don't respond to normal feedback.

Books, Web Sites, and Other Resources

- ◇ **Book of the Month:** *The Landry News* by Andrew Clements: Cara Landry is the quiet new kid in school, until she publishes her own newspaper, called "The Landry News," in which she writes about fellow teachers and students. The people who read the news are shocked to learn how others perceive them, and seek to improve themselves for the better.

- ◇ *Absolutely Normal Chaos* by Sharon Creech: Mary Lou Finney grudgingly begins writing a journal as an assignment for school. Would anything interesting ever happen to her? Begin your own journal. It is a way of giving yourself feedback.

- ◇ www.prufrock.com: By clicking "Journals and Magazines," you'll find "Creative Kids." Go to the home page and check out "Write On." Not only do they publish stories, poems, and book reviews, they also publish your opinion on things that interest or upset you.

- ◇ www.stonesoup.com: *Stone Soup* is another magazine that publishes the work of 8–13 year–olds. You can see their book reviews by clicking "Writing," then go to "Book Reviews." Check out the stories and artwork, too.

Positive Message

"Criticism is something we can avoid easily by saying nothing, doing nothing, and being nothing."

—Aristotle

Copyright© 2007 "I Care" Products & Services (6th Grade)

Reflection Log

Summarize your child's positive interactions during the month and reward yourself for a job well done.

Child's Name _____ **Date** _____

Name of Parent(s) _____

Record the number for each of the following questions in the box on the right.

A. How many of the workbook activities did you do with your child?

B. How many positive recognitions about your child did you receive from teacher(s)?

C. How many positive recognitions did your child receive from family members, friends, etc.?

D. How many positive recognitions did your child receive from you, the parent(s)?

Responsive to Feedback

Positive Activities

D. Record five self–initiated positive activities you did with your child that were not in this month's workbook activities.

1. _____
   _____

2. _____
   _____

3. _____
   _____

4. _____
   _____

5. _____
   _____

Copyright© 2007 "I Care" Products & Services (6th Grade)

What's It All About?

Relationships are built on trust, and trust is earned when people are dependable. When you do what you say you will do, you show people that you care about them. When you don't keep your word or follow the rules, it sends a message that you don't value other people.

Dependability is one of the traits employers look for most. No matter what jobs your child ends up with, from volunteering at the local hospital to being a mechanic, computer technician, or engineer, if someone is not dependable, they will be looking for another job pretty quickly.

Message to Parents

This is one trait you can really influence. When you model dependability, teach it, expect it, give your child responsibility so she can show her dependability and then reward it when you see it, your child will grow into a dependable adult. And you need to do all of the above, because children aren't automatically dependable. They need to be taught.

Dependable

Message to Student

> One way to show people that you care about them is to do what you tell them you will do. Do you want your parents to give you more freedom? Then you have to show them they can depend on you to be responsible. How dependable are you? Why not ask your parents and a few friends? Are their answers the same? Why or why not?

How Am I Doing?

Ask yourself the following questions:

◊ Do you follow through on your promises?
◊ Do you keep deadlines by getting your homework in on time or returning your library books when they are due?
◊ Do you get your chores done without being reminded?

Making Some Changes
How To Develop This Trait

◊ Don't make promises you can't keep.
◊ Be honest; don't lie.
◊ Come home when you say you will.
◊ Talk to your parents; tell them where you are going and with whom you are going.
◊ Always do your best.
◊ Help others whenever you can.

Tips for Parents

Being Role Models

◇ Help your child become dependable by modeling it. Follow through in all that you say you will do and encourage your child to do the same.

◇ Teach dependability by using natural consequences when your child makes mistakes. For example, if she keeps losing her sports shoes somewhere, let her deal with the consequences. Maybe she will have to ask to borrow shoes for the game or buy new ones with her own money if they're lost. If you rescue her every time she makes mistakes, she'll never learn dependability.

Talking It Over

◇ Discuss the following with your child:

▪ *"It's not fair to ask of others what you are not willing to do yourself."*—Eleanor Roosevelt
▪ *Ability without dependability has no value.*
▪ What are some of the ways you can say dependable? *Always there, certain, constant, faithful, loyal, reliable, responsible, rock, secure, stable, staunch, steadfast, steady, sure, tried, true, trustworthy, trusty, unfailing,* etc.

◇ People lose trust in you if you are not dependable. Ask your child to share how it feels when a friend is not dependable.

Dependable

Strengthen Your Understanding

Parent Instructions: Have your child pretend she is preparing for a job interview in which she has to prove she will be a dependable employee. Ask her to write down personal traits she has—or would like to have—that would illustrate her dependability.

Youth Instructions: Plan a "Dependability Day" for your family so you can all practice being more dependable. Talk about what you can each do. Perhaps you can exchange jobs. Be creative in the activities you choose.

Youth Instructions: *Born to Fly* by Shane Osborn and Michael McConnell is Shane Osborne's true story. After reading it, talk with your parent(s) about some of the experiences that prepared Shane to be the person his crew could depend on to save their lives after a forced landing in hostile territory.

Strengthen Your Understanding

Parent Instructions: When customers lose trust in a company, they don't want to do business with it any longer. Talk with your child about how stores try to prove they are dependable to attract customers.

Parent Instructions: Let your child earn privileges such as having a cell phone, going to the mall, going to the movies with his friends, or going to a co–ed party. Talk about your expectations. For instance, if you call her on her cell phone, she has to answer you. Write the expectations down and post them. That way, there is no opportunity for her to say, *"I didn't know."* If she shows she is not dependable, she loses privileges until she is.

Parent Instructions: At the beginning of the month, assign your child responsibility for the well–being of a small houseplant. Have her research and provide the care and feeding needed to keep it healthy. At the end of the month, discuss how dependable she was in following through with her responsibilities. Reward her if she showed dependability.

Dependable

Strengthen Your Understanding

Parent Instructions: Have your child create a picture that expresses the feeling of dependability using a variety of media. The picture can be realistic or abstract. Also, have her write on the picture: *Dependability is* _____, completing the sentence with her definition of dependability.

Parent Instructions: Ask your child to journal about the following questions:

- What personal traits can you list that make you dependable in each of the roles you have in life (son or daughter, student, team member, volunteer, etc.)?
- What particular traits would you like to develop to make yourself more dependable?
- What are the most important characteristics of being dependable that will help you as an adult?

Youth Instructions: With you parent(s), describe what it means to be a dependable friend. Would you always agree with friends or do what they ask? When would being a dependable friend mean doing something your friend might not like?

Strengthen Your Understanding

Parent Instructions: Give your child a hard–boiled egg. Her assignment is to care for her "egg baby" for the entire weekend. That includes naming the baby, making sure it is fed, clothed, changed, safe, and never unattended. If your child needs to go out, she must take her egg baby or hire an egg–sitter. At the end of each day, have her record how dependable she was—or was not—in taking care of her baby.

Parent Instructions: Talk with your child about how important dependability really is, from the making of the space shuttle, to fixing the family car, doctors and nurses being alert, food service workers using clean hands. Research says that 85% of the people who get fired have a poor work ethic: they weren't dependable in some way. Ask your child to imagine he is a manager in a grocery store, the conductor of an orchestra, or a school principal. In what ways would he want the people working for him to be dependable?

Youth Instructions: Here's an activity for two people that requires dependability: outside on the grass, each person takes turns putting on a blindfold and being led across the yard by the hand—while both people are running. The one with the blindfold on has to depend on his partner to keep him from falling or bumping into something.

Dependable

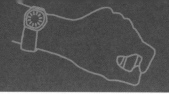

Service Opportunities

◇ Volunteer organizations couldn't run without dependable people. Is your child already a volunteer? If not, help her select a volunteer project she will carry out this month. At the end of the month, sit down with her and ask her how dependable she thinks she was while she was working on the project. The project doesn't have to be a big one. Here are some examples:

- Caring for a neighbor's pet
- Cleaning up after scout meetings, sports practice, or when friends come over
- Picking up litter in the school yard
- Handing out food at the local shelter once a month

If you and your child are interested in a long–term volunteer commitment, go to www.networkforgood.org. Type in your zip code and you'll find a list of organizations in your area that are looking for volunteers.

Scenarios

What Would I Do in This Situation?

You have to select three people to be a part of your social studies project. You're going to be graded on the project, so that means everyone needs to do his best or you might not get a good grade. How will you know that the people you pick will be dependable?

Everyone on your team is working hard on the social studies project but Jason. What would you say to him to get him to be more dependable?

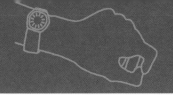
Connect! Connect!

Media/Video

◇ *Thunderbirds*: Enjoy watching this movie with your child, then talk about how the characters were dependable. What were the consequences when they failed to be dependable?

◇ In *Barnyard: The Original Party Animals*, being helpful transformed Otis. Why would that make a difference? How do you feel when you are helping other people? What is it like to know someone can depend on you?

◇ The main character in *Nacho Libre* becomes a wrestler in order to help others. How well did that work out? What were some of the other things he might have done?

Books, Web Sites, and Other Resources

◇ **Book of the Month:** *Born to Fly* by Shane Osborn and Michael McConnell: In this book, Shane Osborn serves as a role model to us all and teaches us how being courageous and self–disciplined can help to overcome adversity.

◇ *Running Out of Time* by Margaret Peterson Haddix: The children of Jessie's village are depending on her to bring doctors and medicine to treat an outbreak of diphtheria that threatens to kill them—but Jessie's own life is in danger.

◇ *The Kids Can Help Book* by Suzanne Logan: Available through amazon.com, this book describes ways that children and youth can make a difference by volunteering in the community.

◇ www.familyfirst.net/parenting/time_management_for_kids.htm: This parent site talks about time management skills you can teach your child to help him be more dependable.

Dependable

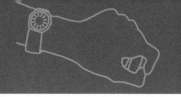

Positive Message

"

There are two ways of exerting one's strength: one is pushing down, the other is pulling up.

"

—Booker T. Washington

Reflection Log

Summarize your child's positive interactions during the month and reward yourself for a job well done.

Child's Name _____ **Date** _____

Name of Parent(s) _____

Record the number for each of the following questions in the box on the right.

A. How many of the workbook activities did you do with your child? ☐

B. How many positive recognitions about your child did you receive from teacher(s)? ☐

C. How many positive recognitions did your child receive from family members, friends, etc.? ☐

D. How many positive recognitions did your child receive from you, the parent(s)? ☐

Dependable

Positive Activities

D. Record five self–initiated positive activities you did with your child that were not in this month's workbook activities.

1. _____
_____

2. _____
_____

3. _____
_____

4. _____
_____

5. _____
_____

Copyright© 2007 "I Care" Products & Services (6th Grade)

What's It All About?

The ability to accept blame—when it is due—is the sign of an emotionally healthy person. It means you're not afraid you'll lose someone's friendship or love just because you made a mistake. When people are insecure in their relationships, however, perhaps because they are often criticized or live with a family where no one acknowledges their mistakes, it is much harder to accept blame. Research shows that children who never take responsibility for their actions or who blame other people or circumstances for everything that goes wrong can become angry and sometimes violent adults.

Then there are people who are always blaming someone else. Sometimes this is to avoid getting in trouble or losing approval. Other times, it can be because the person is trying to show he is the best in the group or the only one who never makes mistakes. Either way, he'll find himself without friends before long.

Message to Parents

Almost by the time they can talk, children blame others for their mistakes. "*Johnny broke the toy.*" "*The dog ate the cookies.*" Little children don't want to get in trouble, and older ones don't want to be embarrassed in front of others. You can help them be more comfortable about admitting their mistakes by not making a big deal out of them and stressing, "*We all make mistakes.*"

You may find that your adolescent is starting to blame you when things go wrong. When you accept blame for things that were really their fault, it stops them from learning to take responsibility themselves. If this occurs, talk through the facts so your child can see that it wasn't your fault.

Willing to Accept Blame

Message to Student

> Accepting blame and blaming yourself are two different things. Accepting blame means you know something isn't right and you want to fix it. Blaming yourself is when you take responsibility for something that isn't your responsibility—like kids who think it's their fault that their parents get divorced. If you're blaming yourself for something that adults in your family have done, talk about it with someone, like a teacher at school.

How Am I Doing?

Ask yourself the following questions:

◊ Do you ever blame someone else to avoid getting in trouble for something you've done?
◊ Do you make excuses for being late, even though you know you played around instead of getting ready?
◊ Do you ever blame your parents when you can't do what you want, when all they are really doing is protecting you?

Making Some Changes
How To Develop This Trait

◊ Admit it when you make a mistake.
◊ Say, *"I'm sorry"* when you're wrong.
◊ Forgive other people when they make mistakes.
◊ Don't take the blame for something you didn't do or cause.
◊ Practice this affirmation: *"Mistakes happen. Making a mistake doesn't mean I'm a bad person."*
◊ Don't make fun of someone else who makes a mistake.
◊ Remember, some things happen that are no one's fault.

Tips for Parents

Being Role Models

- ◇ You can help your children learn how to accept blame for their actions by admitting your own mistakes. Did you forget an appointment? Did you leave the grocery list at home? Those are teachable moments for saying, *"I wasn't paying enough attention."* That way, your children have a model to follow.

- ◇ What message do your words send? If you have a bad day, do your children hear you blaming the boss? Do you talk about how your life would be better if only you'd had a different spouse, different teachers, or different parents? Do you complain when things don't go your way? It's not what other people do that counts the most, it's how we deal with it.

- ◇ When your child takes responsibility for his actions instead of blaming someone else, comment on it: *"You showed a lot of responsibility when you admitted that you didn't study the way you should have."*

Talking It Over

- ◇ Discuss with your child a time you each were too bossy, angry, or upset. *"What happened?" "How did you feel?" "Did you admit your overreaction at the time?" "How would you handle a similar situation today?"*

- ◇ Former U.S. President Harry S. Truman was known to say, *"The buck stops here."* Talk with your child about what that means.

- ◇ Discuss the following quote with your child: *Avoiding responsibility for our actions is the single most effective way to get stuck—or stay stuck—in a life that doesn't work. It turns all the energy we might use for problem-solving into keeping us from the very experiences and information we most need to learn and grow.*

Strengthen Your Understanding

Parent Instructions: In politics, people are always blaming someone else. Sometimes it is because they are trying to get power for themselves. Sometimes it is because wrong has been done. Discuss the following with your child: *On December 7, 1941, the Japanese Imperial Navy attacked American Naval forces docked in Hawaii. President Roosevelt condemned the "sneak attack" with a speech that was actually written a day before the Japanese bombs started to drop. Americans didn't question what the U.S. State Department had been doing up to that point. They thought their country had been minding its own business and was now threatened by Japanese aggression. Millions went to war and died.* How can we encourage public leaders to take responsibility for their actions?

Parent Instructions: Encourage your child to answer the following questions openly: *"Did you ever take the blame for something you didn't do? If so, why?"* and *"Have you ever been punished for something you didn't do? How did you feel about that?"* Share your own answers to the question.

Parent Instructions: Children who are abused by their parents often blame themselves. They think it must be their fault. Talk with your child about what these children must be thinking to blame themselves. If you had a friend who blamed himself for his parents' actions, what would you say to him?

Strengthen Your Understanding

Youth Instructions: Blaming people can be bad for your health. Research shows that when you refuse to forgive someone and keep blaming them instead, it hurts your immune system and can lead to heart trouble, unhappiness, and higher divorce rates for adults. On the other hand, forgiving people get along better with others, have more friends, and are healthier. See if this holds true with the people you know. With your parent(s), make two lists: the first list should be people who blame others all the time, and the second list should be people who forgive and don't blame. In what ways are the people on the two lists different? Is one group healthier and happier? Which group would you like to be in?

Parent Instructions: Sometimes we don't really know what other people think about us. Together with your child, try something really brave. Ask several family members and friends to answer the following questions honestly:

◇ *"Do I ever blame other people for my mistakes? Can you think of some examples?"*
◇ *"Am I willing to take responsibility for my actions?"*

Did any of their answers surprise you? If other people think that you shift the blame, what should you do about it?

Parent Instructions: In *The One–Eyed Cat* by Paula Fox, an eleven–year–old boy shoots a stray cat with his new air rifle, later suffers from guilt, and eventually takes responsibility for his deed. Discuss the courage it takes to admit to doing things that most people consider wrong. Emphasize that taking the blame for a bad action does not make someone a bad person.

Willing to Accept Blame

Strengthen Your Understanding

Youth Instructions: Read *Touching Spirit Bear* by Ben Mikaelsen. It tells the lessons learned by fifteen–year–old Cole Matthews who faces prison or a year of isolation in the Alaskan wilderness in payment for nearly killing someone. He chooses the wilderness, not realizing what lies ahead for him. Cole does survive, but the question is, does he change? What did you learn from Cole's experience?

Parent Instructions: There are times when you have to hold people accountable for their actions—especially if they are public servants, like the mayor, city council members, or a congressman—or their actions can hurt people, animals, the environment, or society as a whole. The way you do this is to describe what they did and the harm it caused without getting emotional about it. Discuss with your child examples in your community where it would be appropriate to share your concern. For instance: *litter in the local river is causing fish to die and no one is doing anything to stop it*. Then, write a letter to the editor about it and send it.

Parent Instructions: Have your child describe in writing two situations in which he accepted responsibility for his actions, and what happened as a result. For example, when he left a party because there weren't any adults there, and afterward he felt good about it and you were proud of him. Also, have him write two situations in which he was irresponsible, and what happened as a result. For example: *when you didn't study for a test and it resulted in a failing grade*. Finally, ask him what he learned from the irresponsible actions and what steps he can take to improve.

Strengthen Your Understanding

Parent Instructions: Read the following summary of a recent sports event and discuss with your child why taking the blame won respect for this quarterback: *Quarterback Jay Davis of North Carolina State University would like to forget the game that ended in only 99 passing yards and three interceptions en route to a 22-14 loss. Instead, he stood out during the post–game press conference by accepting responsibility for his dismal performance against Ohio State. Davis could have mentioned the fact that the winning team was one of the strongest defensive programs, but he didn't. He put all of the blame for the loss on his shoulders. "You kind of blow the game for your team and that's what I did," Davis said during a post–game interview. "Any time a quarterback turns the ball over that many times, you're going to lose."* That's the way the leader of a team should be.

Parent Instructions: If children can begin to think of the consequences of their actions, they are more likely to make good choices. Questions are one way to get them thinking. When a situation arises in which your child is blaming someone else, ask, *"Why do you think you are blaming? What's your responsibility in this?"* or *"What can you do to make things right?"*

Willing to Accept Blame

Service Opportunities

◇ One thing you learn when you volunteer to help others is that bad things happen to good people. Many people need help, not because they did something wrong, but because something happened which they had no control over, like getting sick or losing a job. It's important to keep a helpful attitude and not blame anyone for their situations.

◇ Talk with your friends about how you can help other kids in need. Contact the Salvation Army, Red Cross, or United Way to find out what you can do. There may be a homeless shelter that needs books and toys. You could bake cookies for the local soup kitchen or collect used—but good and clean—winter hats, gloves, and coats that can be given to children who need them. Discuss the different feelings you had while you were doing this. How would you feel if you were in need?

Scenarios
What Would I Do in This Situation?

You promised to go to your friend's party, but your family is going out of town and you're going with them. You know your friend is going to be mad. What will you say without blaming someone?

Your friend failed a math test and blamed you because you wouldn't let him copy off of your paper. How would you handle this?

Copyright© 2007 "I Care" Products & Services (6th Grade)

Connect! Connect!

Media/Video

◊ *The Pacifier*: Disgraced Navy SEAL Shane Wolf is handed a new assignment: protect the five Plummer kids from enemies of their recently deceased father—a government scientist whose top–secret experiment remains in the kids' house. Who's playing the blame game in this movie and why?

◊ *Bobby Jones, A Stroke of Genius:* This is a true story of a man who was the world's top golfer—until he decided to retire at the age of 28. Why did he do it?

◊ *How to Eat Fried Worms:* Being a new kid in school is tough. This movie shows how one boy overcame the bullying and made a place for himself at his new school. How would you react in the same situation?

Books, Web Sites, and Other Resources

◊ **Book of the Month:** *The One–Eyed Cat* by Paula Fox: Ned experiences remorse for his actions when he shoots a stray cat when his air rifle, and he eventually owns up to his wrongdoing.

◊ *Star in the Storm* by Joan Hiatt Harlow: All non–sheep–herding dogs have been outlawed from the rocky coastal village where Maggie lives. But Maggie defies the law and hides her Newfoundland away. A shipwreck causes Maggie to face a difficult choice. Her dog can help rescue the people trapped on the ship, but bringing him out of hiding would put his own life in jeopardy. Would you be willing to face blame?

◊ www.kidscare.org: Kids Care offers hundreds of caring projects for kids to do through their schools, churches, or community centers, as well as charity projects that give families the opportunity to volunteer together.

Willing to Accept Blame

Positive Message

"*The ultimate measure of a man is not where he stands in moments of comfort and convenience, but where he stands at times of challenge and controversy.*"

—Martin Luther King, Jr.

Copyright© 2007 "I Care" Products & Services (6th Grade)

Reflection Log

Summarize your child's positive interactions during the month and reward yourself for a job well done.

Child's Name _____ **Date** _____

Name of Parent(s) _____

Record the number for each of the following questions in the box on the right.

A. How many of the workbook activities did you do with your child? ☐

B. How many positive recognitions about your child did you receive from teacher(s)? ☐

C. How many positive recognitions did your child receive from family members, friends, etc.? ☐

D. How many positive recognitions did your child receive from you, the parent(s)? ☐

Willing to Accept Blame

Positive Activities

D. Record five self–initiated positive activities you did with your child that were not in this month's workbook activities.

1. _____

   _____

2. _____

   _____

3. _____

   _____

4. _____

   _____

5. _____

   _____

What's It All About?

Humanitarians believe that all people deserve respect and dignity. They hate violations of basic and human rights and discrimination on the basis of features such as skin color, religion, ancestry, and place of birth.

According to an agreement that the United States made with fifteen other countries, humanitarian action is all about saving lives, reducing suffering and helping people keep their dignity during and after natural disasters and man–made suffering like wars or persecution. It's also about preventing suffering. There are organizations that provide humanitarian aid around the world.

You probably won't experience the kinds of emergencies that humanitarian organizations like *Save the Children* or *The Red Cross* help with, but in every community there are individuals who are suffering and need help. A humanitarian attitude is part of responsible citizenship.

Message to Parents

◇ We all know how adolescents hate to be labeled. They like to think of themselves as individuals. Tolerance.org reports that they even reject being labeled as "politically correct." They also believe that civil rights is no longer an issue. That means we need to engage young people in thinking about what fair and humane treatment is.

◇ Is your child the victim of intolerance? Nearly 1 in 8 students reported that someone at school had used hate–related words against them. Look for changes in your child's mood, appearance, or behavior. Reluctance to go to school, silence about what is happening at school, or low self–esteem can be indicators that a child is being verbally harassed or bullied. Question your child if you see such changes and talk to school representatives if necessary. Don't ignore it.

Humanitarian

Message to Student

" Accepting people who have different beliefs or people who are from different cultures is part of being a mature person. "

How Am I Doing?

Ask yourself the following questions:

◇ Would you invite a new student to join you and your friends during lunch?
◇ Have you ever tried to comfort a friend or family member when they have seemed depressed?
◇ Do you get upset when you see people suffering from persecution?
◇ Have you ever done something to help people in need, like volunteer to serve meals or collect money for The Red Cross?

Making Some Changes
How To Develop This Trait

Humanitarians don't just talk about problems; they do something about them. Here are some things you can do:

◇ Pay attention to the needs of other people.
◇ If something really gets your attention, makes you upset, angry, or sad, you might be able to do something about it.
◇ Think of some solutions to the problem. Which one can you help with the most?
◇ Ask some kids and adults to help you plan and carry out your idea.

Tips for Parents

Being Role Models

◊ Catch your child standing up for what is right; for instance: voicing support for the underdog, getting rid of hate music, refusing to give in to peer pressure, etc. When this happens, write a note communicating your appreciation and pride, or use some other way of saying thank you that will mean a lot to your child.

◊ Teaching tolerance is an ongoing process. Talk with your child whenever you encounter stereotypes in the media, throughout the community, or even in your family.

◊ Check out your own biases. What are the messages that your child picks up from what you say and do, the people you socialize with, and the places you go?

◊ How do you express a humanitarian attitude? Are you willing to go out of your way to help others, even if you don't know them? Do you donate time and money to people in need? If not, why not?

Talking It Over

◊ Talk with your child about some of the prejudice that your family may have encountered in previous generations– or more recently. What were the circumstances? What did your family do and how helpful was it? How can you avoid getting angry at the ignorant actions of others?

◊ Discuss with your child the following quotes:
  - *The test of courage comes when we are in the minority. The test of tolerance comes when we are in the majority.*
  - *"Tolerance implies no lack of commitment to one's own beliefs. Rather, it condemns the oppression or persecution of others."*—John F. Kennedy
  - *"You must be the change you are willing to see in the world."*—Gandhi

Humanitarian

Strengthen Your Understanding

Parent Instructions: With your child, find out about Mix It Up Day by going to www.mixitup.org. This is a school event sponsored by tolerance.org. The purpose is to help students overcome cultural stereotypes. Read what some schools and youth have done. Then, talk with your child about what she can do to break down barriers of prejudice and learn to better understand people who are different.

Youth Instructions: A humanitarian attitude comes from compassion for people and understanding what they are going through. One way you can learn about people of different backgrounds is by spending time with them. Look for opportunities for your family to visit:

◇ A cultural heritage museum
◇ A performance given by an ethnic group
◇ The house of worship of a different religion
◇ An ethnic restaurant
◇ A meeting, celebration, or parade highlighting another culture

Parent Instructions: Many people are taking sides for and against accepting illegal aliens who have come into this country by sneaking across the border. People should know the facts before giving an opinion. Why are eight million people illegally entering this country every year? Where do they live and work? What would happen to them if they stayed in their home country? Other refugees have fled to America from around the world to escape torture and genocide. Are they receiving the same treatment? This is not a simple problem. What should the government do?

Strengthen Your Understanding

Youth Instructions: The Holocaust is often considered the most vivid example of man's inhumanity to man. Yet, out of the horror of nine million murdered come the stories of the rescuers. These were the ordinary citizens like us who risked their lives to save those who faced certain death. Each rescue story is different. What they have in common is the compassion, courage, ingenuity and persistence necessary to to hide a family for two years, or sneak someone across enemy lines. Go to http://fcit.usf.edu. You will find descriptions of the daring rescues and the people behind them. Read a few with your parent(s) and talk about whether you would be able to do what the rescuers did.

Parent Instructions: In the book of the month, *Walking to the Bus–Rider Blues* by Harriette Robinet, the characters encounter intolerance. Discuss how they were able to overcome it, then share with your child the kinds of prejudice you have experienced personally or seen in the news.

Parent Instructions: We can understand people better if we see things from their point of view. Do this writing activity along with your child: on one side of the paper, write your side of a disagreement you had with someone recently. Then, turn the paper over and write out the other person's point of view. Did it help you understand their side? The next time your child complains about a disagreement with someone, ask her to describe the situation from that person's point of view and how doing that makes her more understanding.

Humanitarian

Strengthen Your Understanding

Parent Instructions: Our tolerance for other cultures increases as we know more about them. Explore some of the artistic expressions of different cultures with your child. Find an art book in the library, go online and search "art" and several countries you don't know much about. Visit a museum or cultural heritage center. Other expressions of culture you can study are holidays, celebrations, food, fashion, entertainment, and dance.

Parent Instructions: Encourage your child to read *The Upstairs Room* by Johanna Reiss. It tells the story of two sisters who go into hiding for several years to escape persecution and death in World War II. Talk with your child about the damage prejudice does to both the persecuted and the persecutor. Also, discuss the courage and humanity of the rescuers who help the sisters survive.

Youth Instructions: Bill and Melinda Gates and Bono were named Time Magazine's Persons of the Year for 2005 "for being shrewd about doing good, for rewiring politics and re–engineering justice, for making mercy smarter and hope strategic and then daring the rest of us to follow." Do an online search with your parent(s) to find out exactly what these people are doing. Do humanitarians always have a lot of money? What about some of the humanitarian efforts in your home town?

Strengthen Your Understanding

Parent Instructions: Talk with your child about who she would name as Humanitarian of the Year. It could be someone famous (but not Bill and Melinda Gates or Bono) or a friend or family member. Ask her why she selected that person and how she will honor him or her. She could make a certificate, give a gift, write a letter, or volunteer work with her humanitarian to help others.

Parent Instructions: You know the saying, *A picture is worth a thousand words*? Go online with your child and find some pictures showing the humanitarian needs around the world. How are the pictures used to get attention directed at human needs and suffering? How do most people react when they see such pictures? Are there needs in your own community that you and your child can photograph and share with others? Perhaps your photos will interest volunteers to collect money or volunteer to help agencies that are trying to meet the needs.

Humanitarian

Service Opportunities

◇ Several years ago, a 13–year–old boy named Mischa got his family and friends to donate money to buy equipment that would help teens who had had a major illness or accident to lead a "normal" life. They were so successful that Mischa founded Kids Helping Kids. Have your child check out their web site, www.kidshelpingkids.org, especially the link that says "How You Can Help." Does it give her any ideas for what she might want to do to help other kids? Talk them over and help her plan and carry out the idea she is most passionate about.

◇ Spend family time helping others who are different in some way from you and your friends. For instance: adopt a family that has just moved into your community and speaks little English. Plan and carry out a drive to collect toys for children living in the homeless shelter. Sponsor a culture fair in your neighborhood to raise money for refugees. Talk about what you learned from the experience, the things that surprised, upset, or saddened you. Then, plan what you will do in the future.

Scenarios
What Would I Do in This Situation?

Your friend Elena is from another culture. She confides in you that some kids pick on her because of her background. What would you do if:

◇ these same kids start picking on you because Elena is your friend?
◇ Elena starts to show prejudice herself because some classmates have a different religion?
◇ Elena begins to withdraw and doesn't want to participate in school activities so she can avoid the kids who are teasing her?

You've concluded that, compared to kids your age from other countries, your life is pretty easy. In fact, you're beginning to think you need to help others who are not as well off as you are. What are some of the ways you can find out about volunteer opportunities in your community? Are there national and international organizations you can contribute to? How would you get in touch with them?

Connect! Connect!

Media/Video

◊ *Hotel Rwanda*: This movie is based on the murder of over one million people in three months. In the middle of this horrible time, one brave man saves thousands by giving them shelter in a hotel he manages. It does have some strong images, but clearly illustrates the needs of millions of people.

◊ See if you can find *Hearts of Humanity* in the video store. It was made in 1932 (that should be interesting) and stars Jean Hersholt as a Jewish antiques dealer who adopts the son of an Irish cop after he's accidentally shot. Jean Hersholt was a hollywood actor known for his humanity. In the 1950's, the Academy Awards started giving The Jean Hersholt Humanitarian Award in his honor.

Books, Web Sites, and Other Resources

◊ **Book of the Month:** *Walking to the Bus–Rider Blues* by Harriette Robinet: This book about prejudice and injustice will stress the importance of tolerance and humanity.

◊ *Go and Come Back* by Joan Abelove: A native girl in the Amazonian jungle opens our eyes to cultural differences as she describes what to her is "normal life."

◊ *Thank You, Dr. Martin Luther King, Jr.!* by Eleanor Tate: This profile shows what being a humanitarian is all about.

◊ There are hundreds of humanitarian organizations in the United States alone. A few are listed below. Go to their websites and see what they do.

   • Action Against Hunger, USA: www.aah-usa.org
   • CARE: www.careusa.org
   • Mercy Corps: www.mercycorps.org
   • Doctors Without Borders: www.doctorswithoutborders.org

Humanitarian

Positive Message

Service to others is the rent you pay for your room here on earth.

—Muhammad Ali

Reflection Log

Summarize your child's positive interactions during the month and reward yourself for a job well done.

Child's Name _____ **Date** _____

Name of Parent(s) _____

Record the number for each of the following questions in the box on the right.

A. How many of the workbook activities did you do with your child?

□

B. How many positive recognitions about your child did you receive from teacher(s)?

□

C. How many positive recognitions did your child receive from family members, friends, etc.?

□

D. How many positive recognitions did your child receive from you, the parent(s)?

□

Humanitarian

Positive Activities

D. Record five self–initiated positive activities you did with your child that were not in this month's workbook activities.

1. _____

   _____

2. _____

   _____

3. _____

   _____

4. _____

   _____

5. _____

   _____

Express Feelings

What's It All About?

Adolescents are bombarded with new experiences. They are stepping out in the world. Their hormones are kicking in big time. They are having feelings they never had before, from apprehension to downright fear, excitement and joy, jealousy, empathy, sadness and depression, even grief. You name it. One of the most important lessons they need to learn is how to identify and handle those feelings so they are not controlled by them. That means learning how to put feelings into words.

When you know what you are feeling but keep your feelings to yourself, you can run into trouble. Other people have to guess what's up with you—and they may guess wrong. That just makes the situation worse. You can't fix it if you don't acknowledge it.

Message to Parents

By sixth grade, the transition from child to adult has begun. This can be a challenging time. Your child may feel overwhelmed by the physical and emotional changes he is experiencing and the pressures he encounters. Parents and teachers expect more, he has a new school environment, peer pressure is at an all–time high, and he is suddenly discovering some of his own interests but may not have the opportunity to pursue them.

You may need to help him identify his feelings and learn appropriate ways of communicating them. When he is not in touch with his feelings, his frustration grows and he may start to feel something is wrong with him, withdraw from you, and find unhealthy outlets for his emotions.

Express Feelings

Message to Student

> Do you control your emotions or do they control you? There are many kinds of feelings. They can help us understand others—and ourselves—if we recognize them and talk about them.

How Am I Doing?

Is your body telling you that you have feelings you're not dealing with? Do you have:
- ◊ a nervous stomach?
- ◊ headaches?
- ◊ moodiness?
- ◊ a feeling like you're under pressure all the time?
- ◊ sadness or depression?

Have you ever been unable to ask for help when you were hurting? Do you get angry a lot? Do you feel fear, guilt, or shame?

Making Some Changes
How To Develop This Trait

- ◊ Pay attention to your feelings. They're there for a reason.
- ◊ Talk to someone you trust.
- ◊ Take time out and think before you act.
- ◊ Do something you usually enjoy.
- ◊ Remember, you're not alone. There are others who understand.
- ◊ Ask for help learning how to express your feelings.
- ◊ Listen when other people are telling you how they feel.
- ◊ Practice putting your feelings into words.

Express Feelings

Tips for Parents

Being Role Models

◊ Since children learn by example, express your feelings honestly. Use "I" statements when discussing your feelings rather than "You" statements. This puts the focus on the behavior and makes the other person less defensive. For example: *"I get concerned when you stay in your room all the time"* instead of *"All you do is stay in your room." "I appreciate it when you tell me what you're feeling. That way, I know how to help you"* rather than, *"You are so silent all the time."*

◊ Encourage all family members to model mutual respect. Do not tolerate "put–downs." If it occurs, stop right away and restate family expectations, but do not "put down" the person who was "putting down" others. Instead, have them apologize and say something positive.

◊ Practice handling emotions with your child. Encourage him to close his eyes; take deep, slow breaths and tell himself, *"I am calm. This will be over soon. I can handle this."* Also, suggest he imagine being in a place that he enjoys—like a beach—or imagine doing something that is relaxing.

◊ Sometimes all you need to do is let your child know you understand. *"I know how anxious you are. I'm rooting for you."*

Talking It Over

◊ Discuss with your child the following sayings:
  - *Music is what feelings sound like.*
  - *"You cannot make yourself feel something you do not feel, but you can make yourself do right in spite of your feelings."*—Pearl S. Buck
  - *The best evidence of what people truly feel comes not from their words, but from their deeds.*

◊ Talk with your child about what emotions are hard to express and why.

Express Feelings

Strengthen Your Understanding

Parent Instructions: Set aside five minutes every morning for a family feelings assessment. How does each of you feel? Are you tired and grumpy? Energetic and happy? Apprehensive? Confused? Recognizing your feelings and making a conscious decision to have a positive attitude can make all the difference in having a good—or bad—day.

Youth Instructions: When we are trying to express our feelings, it sometimes helps to compare them to something we understand. If we say, *"Excitement is like a train moving so fast it's going to run off the track,"* we understand that the excitement is really powerful and almost uncontrollable. *"Get out of the way! Here I come!"* is what it communicates. Practice comparing feelings with some things or experiences. They might be games you play, animals, seasons, or objects in nature. For instance: *"I'm as happy as a lark." "I feel like a storm cloud rolled over me." "I feel as proud as a peacock." "I am bold as brass." "Right now I feel hard as nails." "I feel like a bug under a magnifying glass."*

Parent Instructions: Read *Good Night, Mr. Tom* by Michelle Magorian with your child. Discuss the different ways characters expressed and coped with their feelings.

Strengthen Your Understanding

Youth Instructions: *Dear Mr. Henshaw* by Beverly Cleary tells the story of a boy who must deal with the absence of his father, a truck driver who is seldom around. What are some of the feelings you and your parent(s) deal with? Talk about them with each other.

Parent Instructions: Ask your child what words of a song, a poem, or a piece of artwork expresses how he feels about something. Point out that music, especially, can actually create moods and that changing the kind of music you listen to can change how you feel. Try playing different music until you find what makes you feel happy and relaxed.

Parent Instructions: Talk with your child about how mood swings are common at this age because of all the changes he's going through. Discuss some of these changes and why these changes affect his moods, such as: wanting to be with friends instead of family, wanting more or less sleep, body changes, resisting authority, and taking more risks.

Express Feelings

Strengthen Your Understanding

Parent Instructions: Ask your child to keep a journal throughout the month on the emotions he's feeling. Some of the following questions can help him get started.

◊ Write about a time when you felt like you had to hide your emotions. Have you ever tried to hide them, even from yourself?

◊ Describe some strong feelings you have had. What do you think caused them?

◊ What helps you to share your feelings with other people?

Parent Instructions: Adolescents develop eating disorders like anorexia, bulimia, or overeating for many reasons, but the inability to identify and deal with their feelings is always a factor. Although girls are more likely to have eating disorders, all adolescents need to understand them. With your child, go to the web site below and read about eating disorders, then discuss the questions in the article. Do they apply to your child or someone he knows? Emphasize how important it is to talk about feelings openly.

www.keepkidshealthy.com/adolescent/adolescentproblems/eatingdisorders.html

Parent Instructions: Together with your child, practice using "I" messages:

◊ I feel embarrassed when you . . .
◊ I like it when you . . .
◊ I get upset when you . . .
◊ I feel sad when you . . .

You could also practice adding a "why" statement. *"I feel embarrassed when you . . . because . . . ."*

Express Feelings

Strengthen Your Understanding

Parent Instructions: Pictures can express feelings, moods, and attitudes—sometimes better than words. Using either a digital or disposable camera, assign your child to take pictures over the next week that express different feelings. Print the pictures and have him mount them individually or together, labeling the feelings that each one expressed. Hang them up where you can look at them throughout the month.

Parent Instructions: *The Gainesville, Florida Sun* newspaper reported:

> A recent survey indicated that about 29% of high school students reported feeling hopeless or sad almost every day during a two–week period in the past year. American teens are among the saddest, with 11–year–olds reporting the highest level of sadness.

Ask your child what he thinks about that. Does he ever feel sad or know people who do? Why is that? Do they feel that other people care about them, or do they feel alone and scared? Talk with your child about how to reach out to friends who might feel this way.

Express Feelings

Service Opportunities

◇ To look at the elderly, it's hard to imagine how much fun, adventure, hard work, and perhaps sadness they've had in their lives. They have a lot they could tell—both facts and feelings—but unfortunately, there's seldom anyone to tell it to. Volunteer as a companion for an elderly person, a relative, a neighbor, or a resident of the local nursing home—they would love to have you visit for an hour or two a month. All you have to do is ask them to talk about the past.

◇ Read a series of children's books onto a tape or CD. Arrange for copies to be made and distributed to local hospitals for sick children to listen to. To get started, listen to some books–on–tape from the library and practice speaking loudly, distinctly, and with expression. When taping, give the title and author of the book and leave 30 to 60 seconds in between each book.

Scenarios
What Would I Do in This Situation?

Several of your classmates keep making fun of another girl because she wears old clothes, probably handed down from someone else. How would you feel if you were the one they were teasing? What can you do?

Your best friend keeps making fouls during a championship basketball game. You know he's nervous, but it still upsets you because your team is losing. What are your feelings and what would you do about them?

Express Feelings

Connect! Connect!

Media/Video

- *Raise Your Voice*: Terri wants to go to a music school in L.A. Her brother, Paul, is her biggest supporter, but when Paul is killed in a car accident, Terri's not sure she wants to sing anymore. Talk about the different feelings expressed by the characters and how well they handled them.

- *Monsters, Inc.*: Monsters generate their city's power by scaring children, but they are terribly afraid themselves of being contaminated by children. Follow the emotional roller coaster the characters are on. What did you learn about your own feelings?

Books, Web Sites, and Other Resources

- **Book of the Month:** *Dear Mr. Henshaw* by Beverly Cleary: In the second grade, Leigh wrote a letter to Mr. Henshaw explaining how much he "licked" his book. Four years later, Leigh still writes to Mr. Henshaw, but this time it's about the pain he feels as a result of his parents' divorce.

- *Tiger Eyes* by Judy Blume: After Davey's father is killed in a hold–up, she, her mother, and her younger brother visit relatives in New Mexico. Here, Davey is befriended by a young man who helps her find the strength to carry on and conquer her fears. What fears do you have to conquer? What might help you?

- *The Art of Keeping Cool* by Janet Taylor Lisle: Set in 1940's America, this is a story of a family coping with a dad gone to war. They encounter prejudice, possible spies, going against the tide, and loss. Talk about how harmful feelings can be sometimes.

- www.ncpamd.com/Kids_Pages.htm: For Kids and Teens has articles, games, and book reviews for children and adolescents interested in understanding mental health issues.

Express Feelings

Positive Message

Our feelings are our most genuine paths to knowledge.

—Audre Lorde

Reflection Log

Summarize your child's positive interactions during the month and reward yourself for a job well done.

Child's Name _____ **Date** _____

Name of Parent(s) _____

Record the number for each of the following questions in the box on the right.

A. How many of the workbook activities did you do with your child?

B. How many positive recognitions about your child did you receive from teacher(s)?

C. How many positive recognitions did your child receive from family members, friends, etc.?

D. How many positive recognitions did your child receive from you, the parent(s)?

Express Feelings

Positive Activities

D. Record five self–initiated positive activities you did with your child that were not in this month's workbook activities.

1. _____

   _____

2. _____

   _____

3. _____

   _____

4. _____

   _____

5. _____

   _____

Copyright© 2007 "I Care" Products & Services (6th Grade)

Positive Thinking

October

What's It All About?

Positive thinking is a mental attitude that leads to good and favorable results. Does that mean that positive people expect only good things to happen? No. It means they will deal with everything—good and bad—with an attitude that says, *Things will not always be this way* instead of, *Why do bad things always happen to me?* Positive thinkers don't let circumstances control their feelings.

Positive thinking is not just about saying positive things all the time. It's about gradually retraining your mind so that your automatic reactions are optimistic instead of pessimistic, and that your focus is on what goes right, not what goes wrong.

A positive attitude is one of the most important things you can have in life. It will help you get through anything. Positive people are more successful in work, at school, and in sports. They are less depressed, have fewer health problems, and get along better with other people.

Message to Parents

Before you begin talking with your child about positive thinking, answer the following questions:

- *What was my experience as I was growing up? Were the people around me using positive words or negative words? How did that affect me?*

- *Do I expect to find the good in every situation, or the bad? Do I use positive or negative talk with my child? What have been the results?*

During the month, stay aware of how positive or negative your thinking is. If you tend to be negative, work on your own actions as well as your child's and don't be discouraged if negative thinking doesn't go away overnight. It takes a lot of repetition to reprogram your mind, but it will happen and it's worth the effort.

109

Positive Thinking

Message to Student

> One way to understand how important it is to have positive thoughts is to remember how you feel when you have negative ones. Think of a time when you were feeling bad. It's not unusual for adolescents to be moody from time to time. It's hormones and all the new experiences you're having. Treat these times with a positive attitude: *"I can handle this." "I'm going through changes that will make me an adult."*

How Am I Doing?

Ask yourself the following questions:

◇ Do you worry every time something goes wrong?
◇ How often do you say positive things to other people, like telling them they've done a good job or how nice they look?
◇ When negative thoughts come into your mind, do you spend a lot of time thinking about them?

Making Some Changes
How To Develop This Trait

◇ Use positive self–talk:
  • Keep the voice of your mind saying positive things: *"I can do it." "I have a lot to give." "I can feel good about myself without teasing others." "My parents' fighting is not about me."*
◇ When negative thoughts come to your mind, "catch" them and get rid of them.
  • *"Holding onto anger and hate hurts me the most. I choose to let go of them."*
  • *"Worry doesn't change things. I believe that things will improve."*
◇ Compliment others. It will make you feel better, too.
◇ Smile a lot. It helps you think positively.
◇ Treat other people the way you want to be treated.
◇ Look for the good in what happens, not the bad.

Tips for Parents

Being Role Models

◇ Make sure that you and every member of the family is positive in what you say. Don't allow any making fun, insulting, or criticizing—**ever**.

◇ Make a list of 10 things you do right as a parent. You might do this at the end of the day or over a week. If appropriate, ask your child what she appreciates about your parenting. Focus on things such as: telling your child you love her, complimenting good behavior or positive decisions, thanking her for helping with household chores, including her when appropriate in important family discussions or decisions.

◇ 70 to 80 percent of all communication is nonverbal. Stay aware of what your body language and tone of voice communicate to your child. How positive is it?

Talking It Over

◇ Many young people listen to "hate music" without realizing it. The words of these songs put down parents, praise negative behavior and drugs, and even encourage violence. Ask your children to share some of their music with you. If you hear negative messages, talk about them. You need to balance the negative messages with positive ones.

◇ Ask your child to describe the difference between people with positive attitudes and people with negative attitudes. Which does he prefer and why?

◇ Discuss why most adults believe that some music, movies, and popular groups create negative attitudes in young people.

◇ Discuss with your child the following saying: *I can change my life by changing the attitude of my mind.*

Positive Thinking

Strengthen Your Understanding

Youth Instructions: In *Crazy Lady!* by Jane Leslie Conly, Vernon learns to appreciate people for who they are, even if they look and act differently than most other people. Talk with your parent(s) about people you know who may need your encouragement because they are different or disabled.

Parent Instructions: Positive affirmations are sentences that describe what you want your life to be like. You repeat them many times by saying them aloud, thinking them, or writing them down. Both you and your child create your own affirmation cards with sayings that you can repeat. For instance: *"I feel good when I am kind to people." "This might be hard, but I can do it." "I feel good about myself as a person."* Carry them with you if that will help you remember them. For more ideas, see the book *The Power of Positive Talk* by Douglas Bloch. Your library should have it.

Parent Instructions: Saying positive things to other people can improve their attitude and make you feel good about yourself. Both you and your child make a list of people you can compliment and the positive things you can say about them. How did it feel when you were giving the compliments? How did the people respond and how did you feel?

Strengthen Your Understanding

Youth Instructions: Have you ever heard the saying *laughter is the best medicine*? In fact, doctors believe laughter is very healthy because it increases the oxygen to the brain, reduces pain by releasing endorphins, and boosts the immune system. Doctors have also found that people with a sense of humor are more positive. Spend time with your child improving your sense of humor with jokes. There are lots of joke books you can check out, such as *Lots of Jokes, A World Treasury of Riddles: Riddle Me This, Garfield Swallows His Pride, 176 Stupidest Things Ever Done*, and *Backyard Beasties: Jokes to Snake You Smile*. Ask your librarian for other suggestions.

Youth Instructions: Describe three things that give you a positive attitude and three things that give you a negative attitude. How can you increase the positives?

Youth Instructions: There is a web site in England where you can download "happy posters." The web hosts want you to make lots of copies and give them away or hang them up where people can see them. They've found that the people who make and distribute the posters become happier and so do the people who receive the posters. Try making and copying some of your own "happy posters" on 8 ½– by 11–inch paper and distributing them. How did it make you feel?

Positive Thinking

Strengthen Your Understanding

Parent Instructions: With the fast pace of our lives, we seldom slow down to let our minds rest. Our idea of relaxing is often television with its fast–paced action or music that is seldom calming. Give your mind a break. Go with your child to a local park, hiking trail, or nature preserve. Find a place where you won't be disturbed and settle down for an hour of total silence. Each of you take a pad of paper, pen, and a camera (you can get disposable cameras at the drug store). Write about, draw, or photograph what you see around you. Let your mind wander. How did you feel? Were you able to let the busy–ness fade away?

Parent Instructions: If there is something worrying your child, write it down. Then, list all the positive things that are related to it or the things she has going for her.

Parent Instructions: Plan at least three family meals sometime during the week. Make the mealtime pleasant, something your child will look forward to, by sharing funny events and talking about things of interest to her. Keep it short if this is not a regular event and try not to use dinner time as an opportunity to criticize or put your child on the spot about an uncompleted chore or unfinished homework.

Strengthen Your Understanding

Parent Instructions: Ask your child to imagine that she's grown and has a child of her own who is in 6th grade. Have her write a letter to his child about why it's important to think positively. He can tell his child some of the things he learned while he was growing up.

Parent Instructions: Can you imagine a store that sells fish becoming world–famous without spending any money on advertising? Well, that's what happened to Pike Place Fish in Seattle, Washington. They make sure that everyone who comes into their store has a positive experience whether they buy any fish or not. That's why customers do the advertising for them. Talk with your child about places you've gone where the sales clerks are positive or negative and how that affects the attitudes of customers. What does that tell you about the power of positive thinking?

Positive Thinking

Service Opportunities

◇ Encourage your child to identify and carry out a project to bring positive attitudes to people who need encouragement. For instance, create a puppet play for children who are hospitalized. Check out www.sagecraft.com or www.gis.net/~puppetco for tips on making and using puppets. Other ideas might be clowning for the elderly, collecting toiletries for the homeless, collecting canned food during the coming year for a food pantry, or, as a family, "adopting" a child from a less developed country through one of the international service agencies.

◇ Do you have family members or friends who need cheering up? Make a list of people you can encourage throughout the year and what would bring cheer into their lives. Make a date to reach out to one of these people at least once a month. Put it on your calendar.

Scenarios
What Would I Do in This Situation?

You and two other classmates are selling cookies at the school bake sale. They've been complaining because they'd rather be at the movies. You want to go, too, but you know the money from the bake sale is going to help buy supplies for the art and music classes. How can you encourage your friends to think more positively?

You're really upset. One of your friends is having a party and you weren't invited because she thinks she has grown up and you haven't. What would you say to yourself to help you deal with your disappointment?

Connect! Connect!

Media/Video

◇ *Stuart Little and Stuart Little 2*: A mouse adopted by a human family. Imagine the challenges. Yet, Stuart's positive attitude helps him meet them all. What did this little mouse teach you about getting along?

◇ *Mary Poppins*: This classic movie is all about positive thinking. What are some of the important lessons Mary teaches to Jane and Michael? How does the music help create a positive attitude? Does the music you listen to make you feel positive or negative?

Books, Web Sites, and Other Resources

◇ **Book of the Month:** *Crazy Lady!* by Jane Leslie Conly: This is a story about Vernon, a young boy who must cope with the death of his mother and the struggles of adolescence. Vernon befriends "crazy lady" Maxine, and alcoholic mother with a mentally disabled child. Vernon and Maxine become friends, and Vernon realizes he has the ability to have a positive impact on others.

◇ *Any Small Goodness* by Tony Johnston: Eleven–year–old Arturo Rodriguez struggles to make sense of the world around him. Although his family is loving and his daily life is filled with blessings, some frightening events take place, reminding him that nobody's really safe. Nevertheless, Arturo keeps a positive attitude. How does he do it?

◇ www.pbs.org/parents: This site from Public Broadcasting Service has lots of information and ideas on positive parenting. Do a search on adolescents and teens. Your child can easily link to the kid's site.

Positive Thinking

Positive Message

" Our lives are not determined by what happens to us, but by how we react to what happens, not by what life brings to us, but by the attitude we bring to life. "

—Anonymous

Positive Thinking

Reflection Log

Summarize your child's positive interactions during the month and reward yourself for a job well done.

Child's Name _____ **Date** _____

Name of Parent(s) _____

Record the number for each of the following questions in the box on the right.

A. How many of the workbook activities did you do with your child? ☐

B. How many positive recognitions about your child did you receive from teacher(s)? ☐

C. How many positive recognitions did your child receive from family members, friends, etc.? ☐

D. How many positive recognitions did your child receive from you, the parent(s)? ☐

Positive Thinking

Positive Activities

D. Record five self–initiated positive activities you did with your child that were not in this month's workbook activities.

1. _____

_____

2. _____

_____

3. _____

_____

4. _____

_____

5. _____

_____

Copyright© 2007 "I Care" Products & Services (6th Grade)

Appreciate

What's It All About?

Appreciation means a lot of things: having respect for, understanding and recognizing the value of something, to name a few. We can appreciate a beautiful painting, enjoy the wonder and complexity of nature, the power of the weather, the speed of cars zooming around a track, how we feel when certain people are around, etc. The possibilities are endless. But, real appreciation goes beyond how something makes us feel. It is respecting someone or something for what it is.

And there's a difference between having appreciation and acting with an attitude of appreciation. It's the doing something that makes a difference, expressing our appreciation. Finding ways to say, *"Thank you,"* *"You're important,"* or *"That's beautiful."* Putting a voice to our appreciation is essential.

Message to Parents

Every day, the media is telling your child, *You need more toys, clothes, or gadgets to be happy*. According to one study, parents think this is having a bad influence on the values of their children. Many kids today want what they want, when they want it, and don't appreciate anything less. That's one of the reasons teaching appreciation and gratitude is so important. If we don't, we might soon have a society of people who believe that happiness is based on the stuff they have, not who they are.

Appreciate

Message to Student

" Have you ever heard the saying, *money can't buy happiness*? Having lots of stuff doesn't make us happy—not for long, anyway. Real happiness is appreciating things in life that you can't buy, like friendship, kindness, and beauty. Focusing on what you're thankful for can turn negative thoughts around. "

How Am I Doing?

Ask yourself the following questions:
◇ How often do you take the time to look your parents in the eye and say, *Thank you* for something they have done for you?
◇ When you see commercials on TV for the newest toy, do you bug your parents until they get it for you?
◇ If someone were to ask you what you appreciate in life, how long would your list be?
◇ Check your attitude. When you say something polite, is it only because you should or do you really mean it?

Making Some Changes
How To Develop This Trait

◇ Stop and think about how interesting, unusual, beautiful, funny, or complex someone or something is.
◇ Look people in the eye when you are talking to them.
◇ Use a pleasant tone of voice and mean what you say.
◇ Be polite and say, *"Thank you for . . ."* and describe what the person did that you appreciated. Give a reason as to why it was so beneficial.
◇ Find other ways to tell people you appreciate them, such as doing favors for them or sending them notes.

Tips for Parents

Being Role Models

◇ Take every opportunity to show your children what appreciation looks like. Say, *"Thank you"* to the sales clerk, give your child a pat on the back, be a good listener, express your joy in music, go to the art museum or on nature walks, etc. If cars and sports are your thing, tell your child why you like them. It's more about knowing what you like and why than everyone liking the same thing.

◇ Don't try to force a feeling. Saying, *"Oh, isn't this beautiful"* because you know you should doesn't work. Instead, take the time to look around you and enjoy the moment. If your schedule is tight, at least set aside some quiet time every day to just sit and think about all that is good and what is going right.

◇ As you show appreciation to your children, make sure it is more for who they are than for what they do. *"I love you because you are you."* If your child believes he has to get good grades or behave a certain way to win your approval, he may become a people pleaser without a sense of self–esteem or personal values.

Talking It Over

◇ Discuss the following quotes with your child:
  - *"There is more hunger for love and appreciation in this world than for bread."*—Mother Teresa
  - *"Generosity is giving more than you can, and pride is taking less than you need."*—Khalil Gibran
  - *"Even a mosquito doesn't get a slap on the back until he starts to work."* —Unknown
  - *"The highest appreciation is not saying words, but how we live by them."* —John Fitzgerald Kennedy
  - *The best way to appreciate something is to imagine yourself without it.*

Appreciate

Strengthen Your Understanding

Youth Instructions: Did your parents ever tell you to eat all your dinner because there were lots of starving children in the world? It may not have worked, but the point was well–taken. We have a hard time appreciating what hungry people experience. One way of getting a tiny glimpse is to go without food for a while. Decide as a family what you will do. You could eat rice and beans for two days. Have one apple and two pieces of bread for lunch all week long. When your stomach starts to growl, remember that's how millions of people feel all day, every day.

Parent Instructions: When a child learns to appreciate nature, he develops a sense of awe at the complexity of creation and a desire to protect it. Take walks regularly, exploring different environments. Take a camera and challenge your child to take "interesting" photos that show how beautiful, tiny, complex, orderly, and colorful nature is. Carry a bird book with you so you can identify each one you see. Do you know what all the trees and flowers are? Make it a learning opportunity for the whole family.

Parent Instructions: Practice appreciation daily. Set aside a few minutes each day, perhaps at bed time, and have each person share what he is thankful for.

Strengthen Your Understanding

Youth Instructions: Develop a giving attitude. Brainstorm all the ways your family can give to others on a regular basis. List at least 20 ideas—from meals for the homeless and collecting toys, books, or clothes for those without, to collecting grocery coupons or conducting a food drive for the local food bank. Post the list and get busy.

Parent Instructions: Ask your child to spend 10 minutes writing down things he appreciates about himself. Tell him not to stop with four or five things on his list. It can include how he feels, what he does, the talents he has, and how he treats people. Anything counts. If he has trouble thinking of things, that tells you that you need to help him recognize the positive things he is and does.

Youth Instructions: Appreciation can be developed in many ways and for many things. Knowing the kind of music or art you like and why you like it is one of them. Explore the following web sites: www.princetonol.com/groups/iad/lessons/middle/for-kids.htm: Try any of the links, especially "Art Tales: Telling Stories" or go to Portrait Detectives at www.liverpoolmuseums.org.uk/nof/portraits/.

Appreciate

Strengthen Your Understanding

Parent Instructions: Thank–you notes are still in style. Successful people always use them. But, forcing an adolescent to write a thank–you note may defeat the purpose. You may win the battle and lose the war of teaching appreciation. Instead, let your child select his own methods of saying "thank you." If it's a phone call, a picture in the mail, or a visit, that's "okay."

Parent Instructions: There's a new fad: it's called "junk pile shopping." So many people put perfectly good "junk" in the garbage that many others drive around looking for things they can rescue, recycle, and reuse. That goes along with the philosophy of Native Americans which is to use only what you need. Christmas is coming up. Challenge your child to make Christmas gifts out of found or recycled objects. Go to www.make-stuff.com/recycling/, www.all-freecrafts.com/recycling-crafts/index.shtml or search "crafts" and "recycle" to find some ideas.

Parent Instructions: Hold a family appreciation ceremony. Plan a special dinner at home or at your favorite restaurant where members of your family can tell each other how much they appreciate one another. Have your child create an appreciation award and make copies that everyone can fill out for another family member. Have them present the award at the dinner and share what they appreciate about the person to whom they give the award.

Strengthen Your Understanding

Parent Instructions: Ask your child questions about his music, the media he likes, and the technology he accesses. You may not appreciate it yourself, but you need to know what it is. Talk about how your tastes in music have changed over time. He may be surprised at the things you liked when you were his age.

Youth Instructions: America is sometimes called the "throw away" society because we are always buying things and then throwing them away. People who study this say that advertising is one of the causes. It is always telling us that we need the latest fashion and the newest gadget. Stay alert during the month. Whenever anyone wants to make a purchase, check to see if it is something they need or something they want. Did advertising influence them? What if you put off the purchase for a while? Will the desire fade?

Appreciate

Service Opportunities

◇ Show your appreciation to the volunteers who give time, money, and talent to help the needy in your community. Together with some of your friends, select an organization you would like to honor: a homeless shelter, animal rescue program, literacy program, disaster relief, Meals on Wheels, Habitat for Humanity®, or The American Cancer Society®. You can go to www.networkforgood.org and type in your zip code to see a list of volunteer organizations in your area. Decide how you want to honor the volunteers of this organization. You could bake cookies, send cards, or write a letter to the editor and send it to the local newspaper. You could even volunteer your own time to help out.

◇ With your family, create an "I Care" kit to send to someone in the military. No matter what your political beliefs, it's important to recognize the sacrifices that military personnel make. Many risk their lives and are away from their families for long periods. Go online to www.amillionthanks.org for ideas. By the way, this organization was started by a teenager. Another site to check out is www.operationmilitarypride.org/packages.html.

Scenarios
What Would I Do in This Situation?

While you were at the mall with your Mom, she fell and twisted her ankle. Fortunately, she wasn't badly hurt, but the security guard insisted on calling the paramedics to make sure. How would you show your appreciation for his help?

Your teacher has gone out of her way to help you find out about something that you're interested in. She spent time online looking for resources and even went to the local college library to get a book for you to use. Most kids think she is really strict, but you know she's trying to help you learn as much as you can. How would you help your classmates learn to appreciate her more?

Connect! Connect!

Media/Video

◇ *The Twelve Chairs*: Do the characters learn to appreciate the small things in life? It's a challenge for the former aristocrat who learns that his mother–in–law hid a fortune in the family jewels into one of her twelve dining room chairs, and now all the chairs are scattered throughout Russia. As he sets out to find the jewels, he doesn't know about the priest who has decided to find the chair for himself.

◇ *Radio*: A football coach befriends Radio, a mentally–challenged man. Their friendship extends over several decades as Radio is changed from a shy, tormented man into an inspiration in his community through the power of appreciation. Why would being appreciated make such a difference in his life?

Books, Web Sites, and Other Resources

◇ **Book of the Month:** *The Janitor's Boy* by Andrew Clements: Jack is ashamed of his dad, the school custodian, so when the principal assigns him to help his dad with after school cleanup as punishment, Jack learns a thing or two. What did it take for Jack to learn to appreciate his dad? How did Jack's example change the way you think about your own parents?

◇ *Harvey Angell* by Hendry Diana: When Henry becomes an orphan, he goes to live in Aunt Agatha's boarding house. There, he encounters sad boarders and the mysterious Harvey Angell who has interesting plans for everyone. What lessons in appreciation did you learn from each of the characters in this book?

◇ www.audubon.org: On this site for the Audubon Society, you'll find ideas for exploring the wonder of nature. Check it out!

◇ www.nga.gov: This is the National Gallery of Art site. Click on "NGA Kids" to enjoy some guided tours into the world of art.

Appreciate

Positive Message

"The more one does and sees and feels, the more one is able to do, and the more genuine one's appreciation of fundamental things like home, and love, and understanding companionship."

—Amelia Earhart

Appreciate

Reflection Log

Summarize your child's positive interactions during the month and reward yourself for a job well done.

Child's Name _____ **Date** _____

Name of Parent(s) _____

Record the number for each of the following questions in the box on the right.

A. How many of the workbook activities did you do with your child? ☐

B. How many positive recognitions about your child did you receive from teacher(s)? ☐

C. How many positive recognitions did your child receive from family members, friends, etc.? ☐

D. How many positive recognitions did your child receive from you, the parent(s)? ☐

Appreciate

Positive Activities

D. Record five self–initiated positive activities you did with your child that were not in this month's workbook activities.

1. _____

   _____

2. _____

   _____

3. _____

   _____

4. _____

   _____

5. _____

   _____

Copyright© 2007 "I Care" Products & Services (6th Grade)

What's It All About?

People know your standards by what you do, not by what you say. What are standards? They are what is acceptable. There are standards for how well things are made and how well things are done. Before leaving the factory, clothes are supposed to meet quality standards. If they don't, they become the "seconds" we buy at outlet stores and discount stores. There are standards for food quality, the air we breathe, and the water we drink. There are standards for how well people are supposed to do their jobs: doctors, teachers, auto mechanics . . . everyone.

Personal standards are the attitudes and behaviors we want to live by. If we have personal standards, we know what we want and what we don't want in life. We know the kind of person we want to be. People who are winners—whether they are athletes, actors, or astronauts—set standards for how hard they study and practice. The higher the standards, the better the life and the fewer problems we have.

Message to Parents

◇ Make sure you know your child's friends because they may be a big influence on the choices your child makes. Can you name your child's five closest friends, their ages, the names of their parents, and the kinds of relationships they have with your child? How does the "popular" crowd at your child's school behave? How do they influence your child? If your child's friends do not share your family values, how can you balance their influence?

◇ Help your child be realistic about her standards and not too hard on herself if she doesn't meet them all the time. Children are not always the best judges of what they can or should accomplish and may set goals too high—or not high enough. The key is for her to know if she is doing her best, not someone else's best.

Set Personal Standards

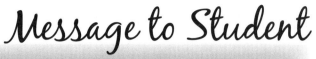

Message to Student

> How do baseball players or dancers, auto mechanics or surgeons get really good at what they do? Sure, they practice. But it's more than that. They set high standards, and when they practice, they don't do something the same way over and over. They try to do it better and better. They say, *"I want to do the best I can do."* They soon discover that they are capable of much more than they imagined.

How Am I Doing?

Ask yourself the following questions:

⬥ Who has personal standards: the person who does something because her friends are doing it, or the person who doesn't?

⬥ If you are with someone who is shoplifting, do you keep quiet because you don't know what to do?

⬥ Do you put up with things just so people will like you?

Making Some Changes
How To Develop This Trait

⬥ Tell the truth even when you might get into trouble.

⬥ Treat people with kindness.

⬥ Decide what you are willing to put up with. Do you want to be the best you can be?

⬥ Make a list of people you admire. How are they alike? What would you need to do to be more like them?

⬥ Do a little better or a little more tomorrow than you did today.

Copyright© 2007 "I Care" Products & Services (6th Grade)

Set Personal Standards

Tips for Parents

Being Role Models

◊ Our standards communicate what we believe about how we should live and how we want to be treated by others. People know our standards by what we do, not by what we say.

◊ Make sure that your family values have been explained to your child and expectations are consistently applied. You can separate the negotiables like allowance, bedtime, curfew, or clothing from the non–negotiables, such as being polite, telling the truth, no drugs, alcohol, or sex, or keeping you informed of where she is at all times. Praise your child for upholding family standards.

◊ One way to model high standards is in the respect you show your child. As she is testing her independence, keep communication positive by setting ground rules. In discussions, for instance, avoid loud voices or name–calling. Each person should be quiet and listen while the other is talking.

Talking It Over

◊ Statistics say that only 25 percent of adolescents reported that adults talk with them about their personal values, and that because parents are reluctant to have children learn from their mistakes, children's values are determined by media messages. Share with your child some of the mistakes you made as a youth and how—knowing what you know now—your personal standards would be different.

◊ To set high standards for ourselves, it is necessary to know what high standards are. For instance, in art, we can look at great paintings or in literature read great poetry or award–winning fiction. Talk with your child about how she could find out what the standards are for something she is interested in. Some examples are: soccer, football, gymnastics, horseback riding, poetry, etc. Of course, you wouldn't try to meet adult standards if you are 12 or 13, but it is helpful to know what those standards are.

Set Personal Standards

Strengthen Your Understanding

Parent Instructions: Challenge your child to collect examples of youths who have set high standards for themselves and who have done extraordinary things. Go to www.buildabear.com/aboutus/community/huggableheroes to see some examples. Each young "huggable hero" sets standards for him or herself and is a role model for others. Talk with your child about what she might do to make a difference in her neighborhood, school, or community.

Parent Instructions: Ask your child to make a list of 5 people she really admires. They can be famous people, family, or friends. Ask her what she admires about each one. Do these people have high personal standards? Can you tell what the standards are by what they do? What do you think the standards are?

Parent Instructions: *The Story of George Washington Carver* by Eva Moore tells about a man who was born a slave and grew to become one of the most well–known scientists of his day. Read the book with your child and talk about what inspired young George to study science, and how he overcame the obstacles he must have faced.

Strengthen Your Understanding

Youth Instructions: Read from *Bill Gates* by Jeanne M. Lesinski how Bill Gates established standards for himself and eventually became the richest man in the world, even though he never graduated from college.

Parent Instructions: Ask your child to select one school subject and set a standard she wants to reach during the month. For instance, getting fewer corrections for careless mistakes, using more resources in a research project, completing homework faster, or keeping a daily journal. Have her write down her expectations, record progress midway and at the end of the month, discuss how successful she was.

Parent Instructions: With your child, check out some of the websites that discuss safe use of the internet, such as www.netsmartz.org, www.safekids.com, or www.childdevelopmentinfo.com and search "internet." Read and discuss their advice, then together develop family standards for the use of the internet.

Set Personal Standards

Strengthen Your Understanding

Parent Instructions: Ask your child to write a set of standards for 6th graders to live by. Encourage her to include attitudes and behaviors for home and school.

Parent Instructions: One definition of the word standard is "flag." Ships often refer to the flag they fly as their standard. In days past, when a horse calvary or army battalion went into battle, they would have their standard flying high. Each battalion had a different standard, one with colors or pictures that represented them. Brainstorm with your child symbols she could use to represent who she is and provide the materials she needs to create a standard of her own. She might include colors and symbols that tell about her personal standards. Go to www.enchantedlearning.com/geography/flags/colors.shtml and search the colors and symbols used in flags. You'll see many examples.

Parent Instructions: Standing up for something means you have standards. Ask your middle–schooler what issue she would be willing to take a stand on, even if it meant losing friends. How about bullying, or vandalism? Would she argue that shoplifting or littering is wrong? If there aren't any issues she can think of, why not? Ask her to write for 15 to 20 minutes explaining how she feels about the issue or why she has no issue she'd stand up for. Talk over what she wrote.

Strengthen Your Understanding

Youth Instructions: More and more schools are requiring that their students wear uniforms because they believe that kids these days pay more attention to what they and their friends wear than they do to learning. Write a letter to the editor of your local newspaper expressing your opinion about this. Are schools trying to establish standards? Are they justified?

Parent Instructions: Following are sayings written by 13 year–olds. Have your child write two sayings about setting and/or sticking to personal standards. Discuss these and hang them where you can refer to them during the month.

- *"Soon enough, we'll look back on our tears and laugh, and they'll seem so small, all those problems, but for now just try to get through."*

- *"Do it, because if you don't try to succeed, someone else will."*

- *"To be who you are is to be enough. To share who you are is to share enough. To do what you love is to do enough."*

Set Personal Standards

Service Opportunities

◇ Set the standard for others: littering is not OK. Recruit some friends to help with a clean–up campaign at your school. Some possibilities might be picking up litter before and after school, getting parents to donate shrubs to plant on the school grounds, painting over graffiti, or making anti–litter posters to hang in the halls. Was it hard finding people to help you? Why or why not? How well do you think your friends understand the importance of not littering?

◇ Create a puppet show that teaches preschool children safety standards such as pedestrian crossing, playground rules, wearing bicycle helmets, or wearing seat belts at all times. Make arrangements to present the show at the local day care center, an after–hours program, or at your house of worship. How did the children react to your puppet show? How did that make you feel? Why did it make you feel that way? You can find out about making and using puppets at www.sagecraft.com or www.gis.net/~puppetco.

Scenarios
What Would I Do in This Situation?

You and your mother have an understanding that unless you have some activity specifically planned in advance or some special occasion arises and you call your mother, you are to come home right after school. Recently, you worried your mother by staying after school for a practice without telling her where you were or what you were doing. What should she do?

Your friends like to listen to music that promotes violence and hate. You can see it's beginning to influence them because they are using some of the language in the songs when talking to each other. What would you do? How could you encourage them to stop listening to it? What if they refused?

Connect! Connect!

Media/Video

◇ Setting standards can be hard to do. After watching *Nanny McPhee*, talk with your child about how she would establish discipline within a family like the Browns.

◇ Some people think that you have to sacrifice a lot when you have personal goals, like athletes who give up time with their friends to practice. Other times, having personal standards means having to stand up to people for what you believe. Watch *Where the Red Fern Grows* with your child and talk about what the boy in the story faced because of his personal standards.

Books, Web Sites, and Other Resources

◇ **Book of the Month:** *The Story of George Washington Carver* by Eva Moore: George Washington Carver is one of the most well–known scientists of his time. Read his story from childhood to adulthood to see how his personal standards made him achieve his goals and overcome being born into slavery.

◇ *The Wreckers* by Iain Lawrence: Some people have no standards at all. After reading about the community that lured storm–tossed ships to crash upon the sharp rocks of their shore so they could loot the wreckage of dead sailors' belongings, talk about why people might think that was acceptable. What was the quality of their lives as a result?

◇ www.kidshelpingkids.com: This organization encourages kids to work as volunteers and recognize the huge difference they can make in the lives of other kids.

◇ www.thekidshalloffame.com: This site spotlights extraordinary positive achievements of kids from around the world. If these kids can achieve such amazing goals, so can you.

Set Personal Standards

Positive Message

"*Have a bias toward action—let's see something happen now. You can break that big plan into small steps and take the first step right away.*"

—Indira Ghandi

Set Personal Standards

Reflection Log

Summarize your child's positive interactions during the month and reward yourself for a job well done.

Child's Name _____ **Date** _____

Name of Parent(s) _____

Record the number for each of the following questions in the box on the right.

A. How many of the workbook activities did you do with your child? ☐

B. How many positive recognitions about your child did you receive from teacher(s)? ☐

C. How many positive recognitions did your child receive from family members, friends, etc.? ☐

D. How many positive recognitions did your child receive from you, the parent(s)? ☐

Set Personal Standards

Positive Activities

D. Record five self–initiated positive activities you did with your child that were not in this month's workbook activities.

1. _____

_____

2. _____

_____

3. _____

_____

4. _____

_____

5. _____

_____

Copyright© 2007 "I Care" Products & Services (6th Grade)

Recommended Books

To order a set of books that corresponds to each month's **Book of the Month** in this Workbook, or to order additional Workbooks from the "Unleash the Greatness in Your Child" Series or "I Care" books (see following pages), fill out the order form below. Then, cut the form along the dotted line and tear out the card along the perforation. Send the card along with check, money order, or credit card information in an envelope and mail it to the address shown on the card. You can also place your order at www.icarenow.com/parents.html, or e–mail the information requested on the card to parents8@icarenow.com.

6th Grade Book Pack   **$55.95**

Saving Lilly
The Girls
A Single Shard
A Week in the Woods
The Landry News
Born to Fly
One–Eyed Cat
Walking to the Bus–Rider Blues
Dear Mr. Henshaw
Crazy Lady!
The Janitor's Boy
The Story of George Washington Carver

	$55.95
Tax @ 7%	$3.92
S & H @ 10%	$5.60
Total:	**$65.47**

	Quantity	Price	Total	Method of Payment:
6th Grade Book Pack		**$55.95**		☐ Check
"Unleash the Greatness In Your Youth" Workbook Series		**$19.95**		☐ Money Order
Indicate Grade Level				☐ Credit Card
"I Care" Parental Involvement— Engaging Parents to Improve Student Performance Book		**$14.95**		
☐ English _____		Subtotal		Name on Card
☐ Spanish _____		Tax @ 7%		Credit Card Number
		S & H @ $5.00 or 10% (whichever is greater)		
		Grand Total		Expiration Date

"Unleash the Greatness in Your Youth" Workbook Series

$19.⁹⁵/ea.

Workbook Grade Level	Available English/Spanish
Toddler	Now/TBD*
Pre–Kindergarten	Now/February 2007
Kindergarten	Now/February 2007
1st Grade	Now/February 2007
2nd Grade	Now/February 2007
3rd Grade	Now/February 2007
4th Grade	Now/TBD*
5th Grade	Now/TBD*
6th Grade	Now/TBD*
7th Grade	TBD*/TBD*
8th Grade	TBD*/TBD*
9th Grade	TBD*/TBD*
10th Grade	TBD*/TBD*
11th Grade	TBD*/TBD*
12th Grade	TBD*/TBD*

*TBD: To Be Determined

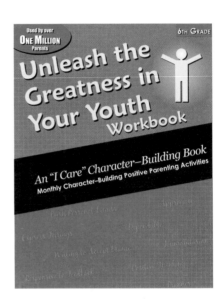

	$19.95
Tax @ 7%	$1.40
S & H @ $5.00 or 10% (whichever is greater)	$5.00
Total:	**$26.35**

- -

Mail to:

Name

Street Address

City   State   ZIP

Telephone (Optional)

E-mail Address (Optional)

**"I Care" Parenting Manual
P.O. Box 492
510 W. Forsyth St.
Americus, GA 31709**

50 Ways Parents Can Say "I Care"

1. Post & Discuss Positive Messages
2. Attend Teacher/Parent Conferences
3. Take Family Portraits
4. Post Affirmation Pledges
5. Eat Meals Together
6. Post Daily Schedule
7. Assign Chores
8. Make Scrapbooks Together
9. Cook Meals Together
10. Award Certificates
11. Watch Movies Together
12. Visit Theme Parks
13. Volunteer at School
14. Read Books to Each Other
15. Attend Family Events
16. Give Parties for Special Occasions
17. Schedule Board Game Nights
18. Visit the Zoo
19. Help with a Class Project
20. Monitor TV Programs
21. Attend Parenting Workshops
22. Send Get Well Cards to Friends & Family
23. Lunch with Mom
24. Lunch with Dad
25. Encourage Hobbies
26. Attend Sport Events
27. Attend Local Theatre
28. Provide Enrichment Activities
29. Schedule Ice Cream Socials
30. Visit the Library
31. Go Shopping Together
32. Attend Friends' Events
33. Help with Homework
34. Post a Child Affirmation Pledge
35. Enroll Child in Book Club
36. Go Fishing Together
37. Go Skating Together
38. Encourage Creativity
39. Discuss Child's Day
40. Praise Good Efforts
41. Say *I Love You* Often
42. Write Notes to Recognize Achievement
43. Document Positive Activities
44. Talk About Positive Activities
45. Role Model Desired Behaviors
46. Support Extracurricular Activities
47. Schedule Family Nights
48. Attend Community Events
49. Help with School Projects
50. Set Limits

"I Care" Parental Involvement—Engaging Parents to Improve Student Performance, by Elbert D. Solomon, is full of research–based, field–tested implementation practices and measurement tools and introduces an innovative curricular approach to parental involvement that will delight parents, teachers, and students. More importantly, it will improve student performance, help parents to initiate more positive activities with their children at home, and enable educators to get beyond the difficulties of involving parents. Available in English and Spanish.

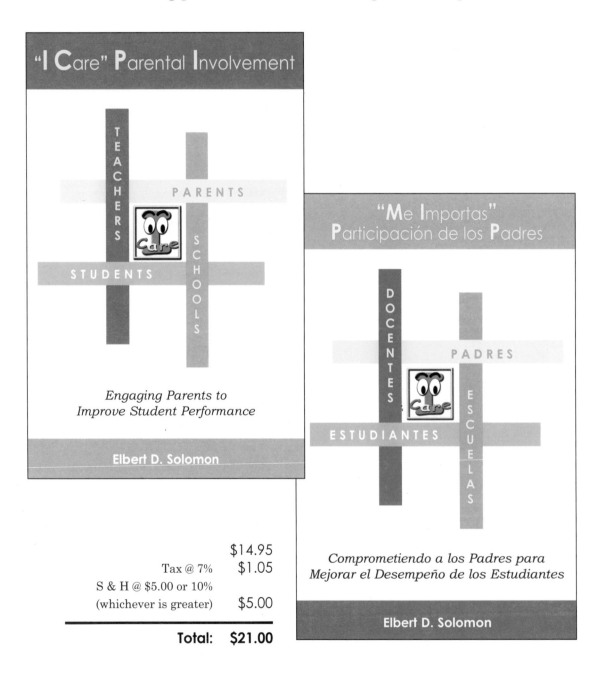

$14.95
Tax @ 7% $1.05
S & H @ $5.00 or 10%
(whichever is greater) $5.00

Total: $21.00